Children of the Stars

Advice for Parents and Star Children

by
Nikki Pattillo

Library of Congress Cataloging-in-Publication Data
Pattillo, Nikki 1966-
"Children of the Stars"
by Nikki Pattillo
A guide to understanding and caring for the new children coming to Earth.
1. Star Children 2. Metaphysics 3. New Vibrational Frequencies
I. Pattillo, Nikki 1966 -   II. Title

Library of Congress Catalog Number: 2008933557
ISBN: 978-1-886940-536
Cover Art and Layout by www.enki3d.com
Book Design: Julia Degan
Book Set in: Times New Roman, Patrick

Published by

OZARK MOUNTAIN PUBLISHING

PO Box 754
Huntsville, AR 72740

www.ozarkmt.com
Printed in the United States of America

Acknowledgments

I could not have written this book without specific people being in my life. Thank you to my husband Charlie for his unwavering love and support. You believed in me, my talent, and my psychic abilities when others didn't believe. To Maddy, who was a sister in another life and agreed to come back as my daughter in this life and be my energy support, inspiration, and rock of Gibraltar while I try and help the world through writing.

Thanks to Dr. Jamey Summerfield and her naturopathy practice that has kept me healthy by improving the quality of my body and therefore my spirit.

Special thanks to Dr. Yong Shu Yang, Alan Yang, and Ivy Yang for YSY Therapy that has kept me healthy through their alternative medicine Qi Gong. Dr. Yang and Allen are miracle workers and I hope the world continues to embrace alternative medicine in their lives.

To my best friend and animal communicator Myra Logan, words cannot describe how grateful the day was that you appeared in my life. Thank you for your love, support, and guidance. I am proud to call you my friend.

Lastly, I could not have written this book without my angels and guides who come to me giving me messages of hope and inspiration to share with all that will walk a spiritual path. I am so grateful to all of them for being in my life, protecting me, healing me, loving me, and letting me know that I am never alone.

Table of Contents

Star Children - Definition

Star children are children who have been sent here from all areas of the universe to help the earth and the people on it. They possess psychic, spiritual, and other extra sensory abilities. These children will bring peace, topple corrupt systems, and shift dimensional consciousness in the years to come. They have come here on special assignment to assist in this rebirth into a higher dimensional earth.

Note to Parents

Since the beginning of time, parents have wished their kids came with an owner's manual. Big changes are coming as this is a new world, a new energy grid, and the children of the stars, or Star children as we call them, have finally arrived to help save the earth with no owner's manual.

Save the earth? Why would we need to save the earth, you might ask? What we need to do is lock all of our parents up in the basement. We'll call it the dungeon to make ourselves happy. So, all we have to do is lock our parents up in the dungeon and everything will work out just fine. Except for one thing, we need our parents to go to work and make money so we can have toys, knick-knacks, pay the mortgage, and such. So we can't really lock them up in the dungeon at all. The earth needs saving by souls with a higher dimensional consciousness who can unite everyone into the belief of global oneness. By raising our vibrational frequencies, these special Star children, along with other light workers, can help spread peace throughout the world and raise our level of consciousness and connect our heart chakras.

Children should be allowed to give parents a time out, ground them, withhold their allowances, take away their cars, or not allow them to have dessert for not being able to communicate with or believe in angels, guides, fairies, leprechauns, and others.

This book is a guide to help parents understand their Star children and to help each parent spiritually understand what is happening with these gifted youngsters who are here to help us. Yes, your children can be your spiritual advisors and they are here to help us. They will try to teach us many lessons. Most we won't understand, some we won't even know are lessons. With the help of this guide, a few of us may catch on.

Do your star child a favor. When he or she has a friend they want to invite to dinner (nudge, nudge, wink, wink), please set a place for them. Are you catching on a little here? This may be their guide, angel, or even a fairy that has dropped in to say hello. You may not be able to see or hear this guest, just know that the guest is there. Yes, I mean REALLY there!

This book is also intended to help our younger or older Star children understand and not be afraid of what they are seeing or hearing that many others cannot see or hear. It is very scary, frightening, lonely, shocking, and harrowing to see and hear things that others cannot. This may include ghosts that may be terrorizing children without parents even knowing it. If a bully at school was mentally or physically beating up on your child, you would certainly visit the principal's office to get things straightened out. With ghosts, angels, guides, and others, there is no office to go to. The children's experiences are real. The ghosts, angels, and guides are real. Understanding this will help take the fear out of these experiences for everyone by understanding our special children, their personalities, and their gifts.

Chapter 1
Indigo Children

Usually when people are sad, they don't do anything. They just cry over their condition. But when they get angry, they bring about a change...Malcolm X

Star children are different, thank God. As of now, our Star children have been divided into three categories: Indigo, Crystal, and Rainbow. Star children have chosen specific parents who will help them develop their natural abilities. So if you are a parent of a child you know is different, your child probably chose you to help them help others in their spiritual path. How lucky you are to be the chosen parent of one of these incredibly gifted souls here to help this earth.

The term Indigo Child was coined 17 years ago by Nancy Ann Tappe, a parapsychologist who developed a system for classifying people's personalities according to the hue of their auras described in her 1982 book, *Understanding Your Life Through Colors*. According to her, auras have been entering and exiting Earth throughout history. For example, aura colors such as fuchsia and magenta disappeared from the gene pool 100 years ago and new colors began making an appearance.

Indigo children have been incarnating on the Earth for the last 100 years. After World War II, a significant number were born, and these are the Indigo adults of today. However, in the 1970s the first major wave of Indigos was born, and so we have a whole generation of Indigos who are now in their late twenties and early thirties who are about to take their place as leaders in the world.

Indigos continued to be born up to about 1970-1992, with outstanding and amazing abilities.

Indigos that started arriving during the 1970's have distinct warrior personalities. They will stand up and fight for what they think is right and what they believe in. They also know when they are being lied to and manipulated and will not comply with any system that may be limiting or dysfunctional. Indigos also have little or no tolerance for dishonesty. They are here to show us that the archaic systems in schools, government, parenting, and healthcare are not healthy and must change or we will continue to fail globally as a civilization.

Larger numbers of Indigo children started arriving around 1992. In fact, if your child was born after 1992, there is a good chance you have an Indigo child. Remember that this isn't a bad thing, you are blessed to have a Star child, so feel honored that you have been given this incredible gift.

Indigo children are born onto the Indigo Soul Ray of Incarnation and Evolution, which means they have access to clairvoyance and healing abilities, and have indigo blue in their auras. This means they have access to the gifts of clairvoyance and healing. They are also able to access what may be termed the fourth and fifth dimensions of consciousness, while most humans have access only to the third and fourth (see chapter 9 on dimensional consciousness). This higher dimensional access, together with the Indigo Ray soul gifts, means that Indigos are naturally more intelligent, more sensitive, and more clairvoyant. They are also creative and often able to access the left and right brains with ease making them artistically gifted, technologically competent, and adventurous. Their gifts also include psychic and healing abilities.

Remember that your Indigo child has chosen you for their parent or parents. It may be a difficult task, but you have important roles.

2

In turn, your Star child has undertaken the task of raising your consciousness to a higher vibrational frequency.

The Indigo children are passionate in their beliefs, whatever they may be, and it can often be overwhelming for them. These children want to know the truth and want to break down the patterns of traditional thinking. The Indigos have a specific purpose. Their purpose is to seek out the truth and change archaic systems of thought on the old energy grid. They are creating a path and unveiling lies and secrecy to help Crystal children who will see the world from an elevated platform of spirituality and a highly evolved viewpoint with complete and unconditional love. The Crystal children then make the path for the Rainbow children who will help instruct us on how to live in love and abundance in the ages to come.

Many Indigos battle depression in their young lives. They are such beautiful and brave souls. This is because they see through everyone with great intensity. What happens is these young children are told how wonderful life is. Once they hit puberty, they have hormones coursing through their bodies, changing who they are. They may not make straight A's, they don't get scholarships to prestigious colleges, and they don't feel like they fit in, they fight with their parents, and then they fall into a depression. There are no rose-tinted glasses on these children.

Note to Indigos
To all Indigo children suffering from depression, this advice is offered. Never lose sight of who you are. Draw strength and courage from just being able to be yourself every day of your life and know that things will get better, and they WILL get better. Every second of every day, know you are beautiful and worthy of being. Know that you are a blessing to humanity and are here for a purpose, to help us. Draw strength in knowing what your purpose is and be proud of that special purpose and who you are. Your path is a hard one, but you have been chosen because you are a soul who has the strength and the wisdom for this task. This earth and the people on it are lucky to have you here helping us. Never give up on your purpose and keep hope and faith always on your side.

On behalf of parents everywhere, we are sorry that our world energy parenting skills are falling dismally short when connected to our children of the 21st century. With the energy changing, we need to fine-tune our parenting skills and understand our psychic children. This means venturing into new territory that we are unfamiliar with. It is uncomfortable for us and we may be scared. Please be patient, we will try to face our fears and try to help you with your purpose in life. We are not perfect and we are trying hard to do what is best for you although it won't always be right. Find love and forgiveness in your heart and bear with us.
End Note to Indigos

Indigo children have incredible specific attributes. They may act like royalty because they have feelings that they deserve to be here. They have great self worth and have difficulty with authority. They may be unwilling to do certain things and often see a better way of doing these things. They can get very frustrated with rigid systems with no creativity. They may feel alone, different, or even anti-social unless they are with others that are like them. Indigo children don't fall for the guilt trip and

4

are not shy in letting you know what they think or need. They don't care what others think of them. They may also be diagnosed with ADD or ADHD.

It is critically important that if your child gets diagnosed with ADD or ADHD that you don't run out and join the medicated child bandwagon. Medicating these special children will severely inhibit their abilities. This is a really easy option for many parents who just aren't patient or can't handle their Indigo children. Try to look at the bigger picture. You and your child have both previously agreed to your arrangement before you even set foot on this earth. Know that children can be handled without medication. This may be very difficult for some parents, so consider joining a support group or even better, order up an angel to help you! It's a difficult journey, but one that can be made together. The problem with medicating Indigo Children is that it lowers their vibrational frequency. They will be unable to or find it extremely difficult to fulfill their life's purpose at this lower energy level because they can not access higher energy or higher vibrational frequencies while medicated.

There are many ways to help your Indigo child. First and most importantly, respect them. Treat them like you want to be treated and you will have a great start to a good relationship with your special child. Practice unconditional love. In fact, we should practice unconditional love with family members, friends, and all people by opening your hearts. Give your child choices and give them reasons and explain why you have made specific decisions. Never say "just because" or "because I said so" to you child. Let your child make his own rules and fair consequences for breaking them if you think it is appropriate. Don't talk down to them and always be honest. Remember that they will know if you are lying. Don't use guilt when talking to them and don't try to manipulate them in any way. Provide emotional support and really listen to them when they are talking. Respect their privacy and teach them to respect others. Admit when you make mistakes and apologize for those mistakes. Be involved in their lives and use rewards to help them get through frustrating times. Give them responsibilities, choices, and natural consequences. Lastly, appreciate their strengths and be open and willing to learn from them.

A Mom's Story
by Mary Foster

When my son Nathan was in the first grade, he was not doing well in spelling. His teacher took me aside one day and told me that I needed to go over spelling words with Nathan to help bring up his grade, which at that point was failing. That evening, I told Nathan to go get his spelling book. He asked me why and I explained to him that we needed to go over his spelling words. He told me that he didn't like going over spelling words. I told him that he needed to do it so he could pass spelling. He said he didn't care whether or not he passed spelling. I tried to use some guilt with him and asked him, "You don't want to fail spelling, do you, Nathan?" He then looked at me and said, "Mommy, I can fail spelling and I'll still be a good person." --- this floored me, but I was able to land on my feet, and I replied, "Yes, you'll be a good person, Nathan, but you'll be a good person in 1st grade next year." His eyes got wide and he sighed. He looked and said, "You mean I can't go to 2nd grade if I fail spelling?" and I replied, "No." Then he said, very matter of factly, "Well, why didn't you tell me that." We then went over his spelling words.

That same year, I was in a minor auto accident and was about 20-25 minutes late picking up my children, Sam and Nathan, from school. I was still a little bit shaken up, and was concerned about how they'd feel, since I was always on time. I was also concerned that they might be worried about me. I drove up to the side of the school and Sam and Nathan were there waiting. I parked the car and got out. Sam came and hugged me, and asked me where I

6

was. I could see he was upset (Sam was in 2nd grade). Nathan hopped off of the bench he was sitting on, stormed up to me, stood in front of me, hands on his hips and asked, "Where in the hell have you been? I've had to wait on you." My jaw dropped. Another mother who was walking by looked at me and asked if he was always like this and I said no. I told him I was in a car accident, and he wanted to see the proof. He told me never to be late like that again. I asked him if he had been scared. He told me that he wasn't scared, he just didn't like having to wait.

End A Mom's Story

Parents who agree to support and nurture a child of the Indigo vibration have agreed to be the caretakers of a soul that carries a new form of energy to the planet. Indigo children are soul pioneers and their parents have contracted to join them in displaying new ways of seeing things and evolving new energy levels. The Indigo soul's mission is to question and challenge old ways of doing things and create the pathway for new manifestations. Parents of these children have undertaken the task of finding ways to nurture this sensitive and beautiful energy these children have and to assist in developing the advanced gifts and talents of the child as far as they can.

The Indigo children, in turn, have agreed to be the teacher in new ways of doing things. But to do this, they must challenge and undermine the old and outdated authority. They can do this in two ways. First, they will question and challenge every belief system or rule that you or anyone else seeks to impose on them. In this way, they will show you what works for them and what does not. It is up to you as parents to listen and learn, and not try to force your will on them. It is important to recognize that they are trying to teach us something new and we may try and resist it, as it may be scary for us. It is important to remember that we need to let our children pave the way for us and accept the changes that will be happening in the years to come. It is for our highest good to let these changes occur.

Indigo children will also be a mirror for their parents. They will take on the dysfunctional patterns that the parents have. These patterns are usually related to low self-esteem and non-acceptance of self. This is why so many Indigos move into self-destructive patterns of drug abuse and sexual promiscuity. They are reflecting back to their families and communities the self-destructive patterns they have learned from people around them. Remember the old expression that what you give out comes back to you. If you have an Indigo child that is displaying self-destructive patterns, look deep within yourself and understand what is going on in your own life. Consider therapy to help break any bad patterns you may be dealing with.

This is also why so many parents of Indigos struggle with destructive behavior patterns of adolescent Indigos. Such parents should examine their own destructive patterns and begin to live out more loving and life-giving patterns that support themselves and their children. How many parents fill their minds and bodies with toxic thoughts and substances and spend their time in work they dislike, suppressing their true feelings, and not dealing with their issues? Your Indigo child will make you aware of this and will be your guide in releasing your self from these unhealthy habits. They may help you wake up to who and what you are and what you are capable of when you are true to yourself.

Remember there is a "good karma" piggy bank and a "bad karma" piggy bank. Every bad action, word, and thought puts a coin in your bad karma piggy bank. Reflect on how many good and bad thoughts you have during the day. Make your thoughts as positive as you can. This pattern will be reflected in your Indigo children that are mirroring your thoughts and behavior back to you. Positive thoughts and actions will bring you good karma in this life and many more to come, so if you are kind to everyone, especially to those who are unkind to you, you will find true happiness.

There should be a tag that you have to tear off your child after they are born before you can hold them. This tag should read: Caution: This is not a vulnerable soul that needs to be controlled and shaped. Please learn from the wisdom and gifts this child brings you. Can not be returned or exchanged. May the force be with you.

An Indigo Case Scenario
"A Mother's Dilemma"
By an anonymous mom on a message board.

Hi all. I have a 15-month-old son that I believe is one of these "new kids." I love my son completely and could never hurt him or anyone else. But my son is driving me crazy!

I have been around children my whole life and I have never encountered such a busy child. I can not get anything done with him. I can't get him to nap. I can't get him to eat anything except bread, yogurt, tropical fruit, and cookies. He won't drink any milk. I can not get him weaned. He can not/will not sleep through the night.

I know these things I mentioned above are characteristics of just about every "normal" child, but my son takes all of these things to the extreme. None of the parenting advice that I have read, been told, or observed applies to my son. I have tried everything short of running away! I am a Reiki II practitioner (a form of energy healing) and I use it on my son all the time. I even had my son attuned to see if it would help and it hasn't. I have spent hours at a time beaming him with my hands while he is sleeping. I have tried all the sleeping methods. I have tried letting him scream. I have let him wake up for an hour or two hoping that he may sleep in and he never does. I have tried rushing to him to pat him back to sleep. I have tried letting him sleep with my husband and I and none of these things worked for us.

I am dying for a stretch of sleep longer than 3 hours. After 15 months of napping I need some more sleep. I also need to get a job outside of my home to help support my family but I can't with the way my son is and not being able to get enough sleep for myself to have a coherent thought puts that idea to a halt.

He is super intelligent. He has a vocabulary of more than 60 words. He willingly brushes his own teeth and does a fairly good job of it. Once he masters something, he never bothers with it again. I have tons of "obsolete" toys, like shape sorters and duplo blocks. He understands Spanish (his father is Hispanic, but rarely speaks Spanish to him). He will follow 2 or 3 part instructions (Where is the remote? Turn the TV on and give it to me). He can open anything. And he sees things that no one else does, if you know what I mean. He has never been sick. Never taken an antibiotic. He has all of his baby teeth short of the 2-year molars. He had his first tooth at 3 months and hasn't stopped since. And he has eyes that can melt your heart.

I am near the end of my rope. Sometimes I have to sit him down and go off to blow off steam. I get so frustrated trying to figure him out. I know he understands not to do something because of the way he looks at me. I have tried explaining why not to do something, smacking his hands, yelling, crying, and removing him from whatever. Nothing has helped us.

I am desperately in need of advice from Indigo parents and other Indigos. I need to learn other ways to deal with these issues. I have read the Indigo Children book by Lee Carroll but it didn't really resolve anything for me.
End An Indigo Case Scenario

Steve Rother (www.lightworker.com) has been communicating for many years with a group of light beings who call themselves The Group. They speak of the New Planet Earth that is coming, and also have a lot to say about Star children. According to them, the Indigos came to shake up our old paradigms and to make room for the next wave in evolution, the children of crystal vibration. At the beginning of their messages in 1996, The Group said that if we could make the planet safe for their return, they would come. Apparently, despite outward appearances, the planet must be getting safer, for recently, they have said that the Crystal kids are starting to enter.

The following selections are drawn from Steve Rother's internet site, where the unabridged version is available at www.lightworker.com/beacons.

"Those that you call the Indigo children have already shifted the focus of humanity. Because of their work and sacrifice, you are learning to make space in your reality for empowered humans. They have done well and will now begin to move into adulthood. As they do, they will shift the paradigms of all that is to follow. The Indigo children have begun the change of your systems that relate to children. Now watch the miracles that take place as they move into adulthood and change those systems as well. Imagine what the world will be like as the first Indigo world leaders take their place. As this unfolds, the New Earth will become firmly rooted in the balanced Crystal energy. You will see space created for empowered humans on Earth no matter their beliefs, sex, or origins. The work of those you call Indigo will be known forever as the great shift. They have come into a harsh world, shaken it up, and are making you re-think everything. These beautiful beings are direct and therefore may have appeared to you as abrasive. Enduring boredom is their greatest challenge. Blessed be the Indigo children for they are opening the door."

Is Your Child an Indigo?

This list compiled by Wendy H. Chapman from her own experience with children and information in *The Indigo Children: The New Kids Have Arrived* by Jan Tober and Lee Carroll.

If you have more than 10 yes answers, your child is probably an Indigo. If more than15, almost definitely.

To find out if your child is an Indigo, ask yourself these questions:
1. Did your child come into the world acting like royalty?
2. Does your child have a feeling of deserving to be here?
3. Does your child have an obvious sense of self?
4. Does your child have difficulty with discipline and authority?
5. Does your child refuse to do certain things they are told to do?
6. Is waiting in line torture for your child?
7. Is your child frustrated by ritual-oriented systems that require little creativity?
8. Does your child see better ways of doing things at home and at school?
9. Is your child a nonconformist?
10. Does your child refuse to respond to guilt trips?
11. Does your child get bored rather easily with assigned tasks?
12. Does your child display symptoms of Attention Deficit Disorder?
13. Is your child particularly creative?
14. Does your child display intuition?
15. Does your child have strong empathy for others?
16. Did your child develop abstract thinking at an early age?
17. Is your child very intelligent?
18. Is your child very talented (may be identified as gifted)?
19. Does your child seem to be a daydreamer?

20. Does your child have very old, deep, wise looking eyes?
22. Does your child have spiritual intelligence?

A Case of Suicide with Jennifer Hoffman

Jennifer Hoffman with the spiritual advice Uriel Heals website talks about Indigos and their struggle with thoughts of suicide. She says that Indigo children, among other children, follow through with suicide, leaving a trail of grief behind them. They have trouble accepting things and since many Indigos have had difficult childhood experiences, their wounds are often painful and deep. Their empathic abilities serve to amplify the pain that they feel and add to it the pain of those around them. Her son had many Indigo friends, many of whom were struggling with their own problems. She felt that he was processing his friends' emotions as well as his own. They struggled for three years with this problem, going through counseling, drug therapy (briefly), and spent much time talking. The drugs seemed to make things worse. In many cases, Indigos can have unusual reactions to drugs or be intolerant of them. Since they are prone to addiction, they can also become addicted to many types of medication.

While her son did not commit suicide, he had several friends who did. It was a very sad and difficult experience for everyone. Each parent whose Indigo child goes through emotional issues and painful experiences needs to understand that their children are unable to turn off their emotions as we have learned to do. They process the emotional energy around them, which they can believe is their own. Since they are highly empathic and intuitive, teaching them how to channel their empathic energy more effectively will help them to understand which emotional energy is theirs and which belongs to others. Effective communication between children and parents is helpful with Indigo children because they may imagine all sorts of things and have trouble distinguishing between reality and their beliefs and fears. Although they are highly intelligent, they also tend to be emotionally immature and need much more support than they will acknowledge. Through several years of talking, working through issues, teaching her son how to focus his empathic energy and letting him know that she was there for him, her son was able to get through this difficult period and is now doing well. It is a challenge that many parents of Indigos face, but one that they can, with effort, help their children through.

Pain, confusion, and frustration are a common theme for Indigos. Indigo children who are in the 18-20 year old age range have a particularly difficult time. Indigo children, who are supposed to be leaving home and entering the world at this time can't because many of them are stuck and afraid to leave. They may be depressed, drinking and/or using drugs, or have simply dropped out and are not doing anything at all. Many of their parents were either in college or married at that age and are frustrated with their children's behavior. Parents are overwhelmed by and frightened at the depths of their children's depression, anger, and apparent inability to move forward or to move out of the black hole that they seem to be in. Can these children be helped?

Some Indigos are intimidated by what they see as a challenge to meet or exceed their parents' successes. Their parents may represent a very successful generation. Others are afraid that they will not measure up to society's heavy expectations of this generation. Some just want to do exactly the opposite of what their parents are doing, not because they are trying to be difficult, but because they want to create their own path in life. Still others simply do not know what they want to do and are overwhelmed by the vast range of options that they have and the challenge of choosing one thing and being successful at it, as their parents may have done. What if they don't like it? Will they be stuck with it?

As a generation, Indigos are very creative, intuitive, motivated, and they do everything with purpose and intention. When they get stuck, they do it well. But they can be moved out of their black hole, with help. One noticeable thing is that many Indigos were bullied by their peers as children and they may have suffered for being different. Whatever emotions they felt at the time, they are carrying with them into their early adulthood. The fear of being bullied or of being persecuted for who they are, how they look or act seems to have re-awakened in many of them. The solution most often proposed for parents of Indigo children is to communicate with them, to talk about their fears, learn where their interests lie, to reassure them and to help them learn to be comfortable with their differences.

The Indigo energy will not conform to rules and regulations. They may not be able to work at jobs or careers that they do not like or that are not suited to their gifts and talents. However, they are creative enough to find alternatives that suit them, if they are supported in their efforts. Rather than being frustrated with them (although their behavior is frustrating), ask them why they feel the way they do, instead of asking them what is wrong with them. This is a challenging situation for any parent, but it can be made less difficult by making an effort that starts with communication. The situation will not be resolved overnight, but it will improve over time. You can help your Indigo child climb out of the black hole, find their path, and blossom into their creative energy.

Indigo children, many now in their late teens and early adulthood, are reaching a crisis point. They are struggling with their purpose in the world, their ability to carry out their mission, and dealing with their gifts and talents. Many Indigos who contemplate suicide do so when they are deeply depressed. They can no longer make sense of their lives or themselves and see no future past their current situation. They do not know how to get from where they are to the next step in their lives. This is a generation that grew up on video games where they had to die to get to the next level. Are they taking that concept into their reality, not understanding its implications?

While the Indigo energy is wonderfully creative when expressed positively, it can be very destructive in its negative expression. That extends not only to the Indigos outer world, but also their inner world. They are often their own worst enemies, creating a host of problems and difficulties for themselves (and their parents). Indigos are a generation that requires involved parenting, where the parents need to be present in their lives in every sense, including emotionally. Most parents are stressed with demanding jobs and lifestyles and do not have time to be there for their children. This is when Indigos get into trouble. They seem to deliberately push their parents away at the time when they are in greatest need of their insight and attention. When an Indigo says, "I can handle this," it usually means that they are in over their heads and desperately need help, even though they won't ask for it and will accept it very reluctantly.

The tragedy of a child suicide is unthinkable, not only to the family, but also to society in general. These children have much to contribute and teach us and parents and families need to be an active presence in their lives. When Jennifer's Indigo son finally came out of his suicidal period, he wrote her a letter in which he expressed his gratitude at the unwavering love that she gave him, even when he was at his most unlovable. He told her that he probably would not be here if it weren't for her efforts. She had convinced him that his place was here and that moving to the next level meant finding the best outlet for his skills and gifts. Together they worked on discovering what that was.

Parents of Indigos can help their children make the decision to stay by teaching them that the next level is attainable by becoming who they are, finding or creating their path, and living it with passion, no matter what it looks like. They also need to learn to accept the love and help of those whom they chose as

16

their parents and spiritual teachers by knowing that they are there for them when they need it the most, whether or not they are willing to accept their help. These children eventually will accept help and the world will benefit from their experiences. They will also teach other Indigos how to get to the next level in their spiritual path by staying on this one. Parents of Indigos can help their children and help them get past this difficult period and make suicide an option that they do not even consider.

End A Case of Suicide with Jennifer Hoffman

The Indigo children are the first generation to help humanity and are now represented in today's teenagers. Indigo children are wise beyond their years. "I know that" is a phrase that they frequently use and while it can be frustrating to parents, the truth is that they do know many things. They are also very perceptive about others and are prone to saying the most politically incorrect thing at the most inappropriate moment. But social conventions are not part of their understanding. They know what has to be said and they are not afraid to say it.

Indigos are having a difficult time here on earth. They are called the Ritalin generation, because there are times of extreme behavior problems in these children that created mass prescription of pharmaceutical products such as Ritalin, Wellbutrin, and Adderal. But does the problem lie with the children or with the system that they cannot adjust to? These children were and still are unable to cope with the existing low-level energies and so did what they did best, they rebelled and created a revolution. The generations before them were accustomed to accepting the status quo. Not the Indigos. They represent the calm before the storm so to speak, because they have prepared us for the next generation of even more evolved children, the Crystals.

Chapter 2
Crystal Children

No on forgives with more grace and love than a child...Real Live Preacher

The Crystal children began to appear on the planet from about 1990-2010, although a few scouts came earlier. Their main purpose is to take us to the next level in our evolution and reveal to us our inner and higher power. They function as a group consciousness rather than as individuals, and they live by the "Law of One" or global oneness. They are also advocates for love and peace on this planet.

They are mostly born into the Gold Ray of Incarnation and Evolution, which makes them masters of creation, especially light and sound. They are born on the sixth dimension of consciousness, with the potential to open up rapidly to the ninth dimensional level of full Christ consciousness, and then from there to the thirteenth dimension, which represents universal consciousness.

Crystal children's auras aren't specifically opalescent, but are octarine. This is a color that isn't in the normal visual range of human eyes, but is the manifest color of high magic, and on another color octave entirely. They have beautiful pastel hues to them. To the untrained eye, it appears to be without color at all, therefore Crystal, but the extremely high frequency of the energy field is what gives it away.

The first thing you will recognize about Crystal children is their forgiving nature. They are very sensitive, warm, and caring. Don't mistake these characteristics as a sign of weakness as Crystal children are also very powerful.

The Crystal child is incredibly sensitivity, which stems from the ability to feel universal consciousness. You won't be able to hide anything from these children. You won't be able to lie to them either, as they will know immediately what the truth is. It is important to mention that Crystal children know what is in your thoughts and even more importantly, what is in your heart. This is another reason why they are so sensitive.

Children with a crystal vibration have the ability to reflect things back to the universe that are of no importance to them. Not only will they reflect this energy back, they will reflect it in such a way that it is stronger than when it was taken in.

Special Note
If you are the parent of a Crystal child, it is crucial that your child take in good energy at all times or as much as possible. Your role is to help these children reflect harmony, peace, and oneness into the Universe. This, in turn, will help all of us raise our vibrational frequencies and help spread peace around the world.
End Special Note

The Power of Crystal Kids from Crystalchildren.com
Imagine that you have just discovered that your two year old son can move things with his mind. How will you explain that to the neighbors? Envision what it will be like the first time you take your little girl out in public and she begins to read the thoughts of the person sitting next to you in the restaurant. Much like the Indigo children that have preceded them, Crystal children have a very thin veil. It will be very common to have a Crystal child walk up to you and say, "Mommy, do you remember when I was

your grandfather?" Additionally, Crystals have inter-dimensional abilities that enable them to cross the lines between alternate realities. We may misinterpret these abilities. Eventually the children themselves will show us how it all works. One of the most important abilities we will see with Crystals is that they carry an inbred understanding of unity consciousness. To us, this will be seen first as their ability to read our thoughts and know what is in our hearts through complete emotional empathy. Even though this will be difficult for humanity to accept at first, it is clear to see that when we know what everyone else is thinking and feeling there will be no more secrets or lies. When there are no more secrets or lies, there can be no place for things like war.
End The Power of Crystal Kids

Just as Indigo children don't react to guilt, you will find Crystal children do not react to fear. Fear is prevalent in almost everyone. The collective consciousness of our earth and universe magnifies this emotion. With terrorism on the rise, it is important now more than ever to let go of this age-old emotion. There is nothing to fear in this life, as all is unfolding as it should. Not even death should be feared, as there is no such thing.

Most importantly, do not fear Star children. These gifted youngsters will feel fear and magnify it back. If you have a lower vibrational energy, you may react strongly to these children with such a high vibrational frequency. Remember that the energy in the universe is changing for the better. As our vibrational frequencies are raised, a collective consciousness of peace and love are emanating into the universe.

Crystal scouts that arrived decades ago came to test the waters for future Star children. These scouts had much grief. They were different and possibly psychic. It has taken our society a long time to start recognizing these types of people and accepting them. We are all becoming crystalline bodies whether we realize it or not.

21

The continued energy shift that is happening is supporting this energy pattern and moving us all in that direction.

This change in energy or energy shift is definitely wreaking havoc in the world. The many natural disasters that are occurring will continue to occur in the years to come as a result of the energy shift. This is part of the shift. It is important to remember during this time that we all must be good and kind souls. Always help others in need, be honest and kind, clear your emotional bodies, and remember your good karma piggy bank.

In time, Crystal children will help us achieve our goals and understand the concept of oneness. Fear and greed are becoming emotions of the past and will be replaced by peace, harmony, and this sense of oneness.

Doreen Virtue, noted author and expert on Star Children, has written about the characteristics of Crystal children. She says these characteristics may include:

- Have large, communicative eyes and an intense stare.
- Are highly affectionate.
- Begin speaking later in life, but often use telepathy or self-invented words or sign language to communicate.
- Love music and may even sing before talking.
- Are extremely connected to animals and nature.
- Are often very interested in rocks, crystals, and stones.
- Are extremely artistic.
- Are highly empathic and sensitive.
- Are forgiving and generous to others.
- Draw people and animals near them and love attention.
- Often have a good sense of balance and are fearless when exploring high places.
- Often see or hear angels and spirit guides - both their own and others'.

- Dislike high-stress environments with many distractions.
- Dislike loud/sharp sounds.
- Dislike bright, unnatural lights.
- Often enjoy choosing their own meals and/or when they eat them.
- Often speak about universal love and healing.
- Sometimes show healing gifts at young ages.
- Don't react well to sugar, caffeine, or unnatural foods/chemicals.
- Dislike fighting or refuse to keep an argument going very long.
- Often show strength in telekinesis (or Psychokinesis).
- Often amplify emotional energies they gain from their environment (such as negative energies).
- Can become uncomfortable when around electrical devices too long (watching TV, computer, etc.), sometimes resulting in a trance-like state.
- Sometimes seem 'clingy' to their parents until 4 or 5.
- Often stare at people for long periods of time (this allows them to read a person and find out more about them through their own personal memories and energy).
- Can sometimes be manipulative and throw tantrums if they cannot create a reality that is good for them.
- Are easily over-stimulated and need to meditate/be alone often to replenish themselves.
- Don't usually have trouble with fear or worry.
- Enjoy discussing spiritual or philosophical topics.
- May appear to be looking at nothing or talking to no one (sign of clairvoyance and/or clairaudience).

Indigos and Crystals work together to tear down archaic systems and build up new ones.

Again, parents of these special children need to realize that they agreed to bring these wise and powerful children into the world whose mission reaches out to the globe as a whole and not just as individuals or individual families. They are also here to work on the energy grids, raising vibrational frequencies to help facilitate global changes for a more peaceful earth.

It is important to support these gifted young children and be cautious not to stress them or put them in busy environments. Like Indigos, Crystal children will also help raise the vibrational frequency of their parents. Crystals have a way of drawing other people with the correct energy to interact in a family's life. Parents of a Crystal child will benefit greatly from these incredible children through their powerful, loving, and creative energies.

These children, with their higher level of consciousness, should be considered equals in families. They should be involved in family issues and be allowed to give options and solutions to problems. Don't forget that they are on a much higher vibrational frequency than many of their parents.

Vibrational Frequencies
Vibrational frequency is the rate at which atoms and sub-particles of a being vibrate. The higher this vibrational frequency is, the closer it is to the frequency of light. Your words and thoughts send out a vibration that attracts an experience of a similar vibration. If you send out fear, you attract fear. If you send out love, you attract love.

Everything in the universe is energy and energy vibrates at different rates. You have a unique vibration, which is the product of all of the influences you have encountered both from present and past lives. The influences you focus your attention on are those which determine your vibration. Negative vibrations are associated with the lower chakras. Negative vibrations include hatred, anger, doubt, fear, jealousy, envy, judgment, impatience, disharmony, imbalance, and insecurity. Positive vibrations are love, harmony, peace, balance, kindness, understanding, and compassion. The negative emotions are not "bad." We all, at one time or another, experience emotions of a lower vibration. These emotions only become harmful when you base your words or actions upon them. You can feel anger about something and still make a conscious choice to act out of love. When you do this, you are raising your vibration from one of anger to one of love. Changing your thoughts and actions will help raise your vibrational frequency.

The fastest way to raise your vibrational frequency is through gratitude. Be grateful for all things in your life, both good and bad. Try and thank your angels, guides, loved ones, friends, and the Universe every day. By being grateful, you will raise your energy or vibrational frequency with great ease.

End Vibrational Frequencies

Another phenomenon associated with Crystal children is delayed speech patterns. The fact is not surprising that delayed speech is rising in children that are incredibly psychic. Why would they need to talk when they can communicate with their minds? It is not uncommon to see Crystal children that don't really speak until they're 3 or 4 years of age. Most parents are in touch with their children and know what they are communicating. These children may use sign language, sing, or make specific sounds to communicate.

Crystal Challenges from crystalchildren.com
Being Crystal means having tremendous sensitivity to all things. This may be difficult at first, yet in time, the Crystal kids will learn to deal with the lower vibrational energies to which we have become accustomed. Much the way that Indigo children have no reference for guilt, the children of crystal vibration have no reference for the lower emotion of fear. Being extremely powerful

and emotionally empathic, if they experience an overload of fear from those around them they can actually reflect it back, amplifying it in the process. That is one of the reasons we are currently going through global processes (terrorism) that will help us deal with our fears as a collective whole.

They also have physical challenges that have already begun to surface. Having loose ethereal bodies to enable inter-dimensional abilities, these children are vulnerable to influences that push them out of their body. This may appear as autism in the first Crystal children. It is suggested that we closely examine vaccines and other medicines that we give our children routinely. They say that the vaccines have not changed. The Crystal children are entering with a higher vibration that makes them more vulnerable. It is suggested that the fact that autism has increased 300 percent over the last ten years in parts of the world where we vaccinate our children, is evidence that the Crystal kids are already entering this world.

End Crystal Challenges

Like Indigo children being diagnosed with ADD or ADHD, the medical profession will also label Crystal children. They will say that they have abnormal or delayed speech patterns. Parents should remember to look at the big picture. If children are successfully communicating at home and not having any problems, the medical profession should not try and make it a problem.

The new generation of children of the 21st century can not be labeled and stuck into a box. Most people are on the old energy grid. It is difficult to try and keep up with the energy and higher vibrational frequencies of the new souls coming here to help us. Some of their characteristics will seem abnormal, but rest assure they are not.

It is important that health care professionals update their diagnosis and become more aware of what is happening around them. It may be difficult to understand energy and realize that we are moving past medicine and things that will pull our vibrational frequencies to a lower level. People have been healing themselves with their own energies for quite some time. This trend will continue and even become more common in the decades to come.

The medical profession should also understand why autism is on the rise. It is thought that the new Crystal children, with their higher vibrational frequency, are unable to handle vaccinations. These souls have loose ethereal bodies and the poison from the vaccines literally pushes them out of their bodies. You can protect these children by keeping their meridians balanced and purging these toxins from their bodies by whatever alternative medicine you agree with. This may include getting their meridians balanced, chakras balanced, energy work, Reiki, homeopathy or whatever you are comfortable with. It is important to purge toxins from your body within 24-48 hours after giving medicine, especially after giving your children vaccinations. This time frame is when it is easiest to purge toxins and allow them to do the least amount of damage to the body. After 48 hours there may be some damage and it will be more difficult to eliminate the toxins.

It is important that both Mom and Dad get their meridians or energy balanced before they have children; however, it is never too late to get energy work done even if you are 70, 80, or 90 years of age.

Crystal children are among the most connected, communicative, caring, and cuddly of any generation. They are also quite philosophical and spiritually gifted. They display an unprecedented level of kindness and sensitivity to this world. Crystal children spontaneously hug and care for people in need.

In the past, the vibrational frequency of the world has not been high enough to support these special souls. The energy shift that is occurring is changing the vibrational frequencies and these frequencies have finally become high enough to support these children.

As mentioned earlier, Steve Rother (www.lightworker.com) has been communicating for many years with a group of light beings who very fittingly call themselves The Group. They speak of the new planet earth that is coming, and also have a lot to say about Crystal children. According to them, the Indigos came to shake up our old paradigms and to make room for the next wave in evolution, the "children of crystal vibration." At the beginning of their messages in 1996, the Group said that if we could make the planet safe for their return, they would come. Apparently, despite outward experiences, the planet must be getting safer, for recently they have said that the Crystal kids are starting to enter.

The children of Crystal vibration are what you would consider to be the magical children with abilities that you may have yet to understand. The attributes of Crystal children are simply two-fold, they are extremely powerful and yet extremely vulnerable. They are highly evolved beings and have an understanding of what simple energy really is. Feats that you would think impossible may seem like child's play to humans carrying the crystal vibration. You will begin to see magical abilities in human children that you have never seen before. Their basic understanding of energy will make it possible to manipulate energy in new ways.

Many Crystal children can levitate inanimate objects with their minds. They also have problems with electricity. Your Crystal child will go through many watches, phones, and clocks next to the bed. This is because their vibrational energy is on a much higher frequency and it affects electrical objects.

At first, Crystal children will tend to gather with other Star children. They will form groups that will grow together, supporting each other energetically. They will do it all by themselves, so parents of Crystal children will not need to worry about finding the best environment for their children. Expect to see groups of magical children with abilities that exceed far beyond the norm. As time goes on, you may see an acclimation of this energy and will become more accustomed to the odd stories that will circulate about the strange new abilities of some children.

The Group goes on to say that what we are beginning to see so far is only the scouts who have been sent ahead to test the waters, and that powerful as they are, they are carrying only the first hints of the energy that is to come. They will be able to read our minds and also our hearts. There will be no more secrets among people. They will have a sensitivity beyond our comprehension, but this sensitivity will be a gift as well as a challenge. The Group continues, saying:

"Unlike the children of Indigo vibration, the Crystal children are so sensitive that they may feel threatened by the harshness of what people are holding in their hearts. Some will find safety in retreating and going within. There are some people who will think this is a sign of weakness and may even attempt to exploit these gentle beings. Let us set your mind at ease when we tell you that exploitation will not be possible. The children of crystal vibration are powerful beyond your understanding. Even though they may have great difficulty understanding and interacting, they will always know their true power and who they are."

According to The Group, their biggest challenge will be their inability to deal with other people's fear. Fear is based on a belief in lack, and these children will enter with a belief system that knows nothing of lack, and therefore nothing of fear. They will need help in dealing with the general fear around them, which means that we will need to start dealing with our own deeply ingrained habits of fear, separation, limitation, and lack.

These Crystal children and scouts will know how to heal. They can also do this for other people. They know of others like them because they can sense them within their own minds, but sometimes feel isolated physically. They are in touch with fairies, angels, and multidimensional cosmic beings. They have a hard time finding people they can trust and have learned that it is not always safe to share too much of their world with adults around them. They have great difficulty relating to the self-centered and limited perspectives that human society operates within. Most people find them very threatening in their vulnerability and directness. They feel frustrated because they know they are here to help, but feel that if they unleash their powers to assist the world, it could leave much chaos in its wake.

Story From A Crystal Mom and Daughter
When my daughter was first born, the most amazing thing about her were her eyes. She has these eyes that look straight into the depth of your soul with such happiness and understanding.

As she grew older, she cared for her dollies, put the spiders safely from the inside of the house to the outside and gave all kinds of gifts and food to her fairy friends outside.

At 3 years of age, she began laying her Dad and I on our tummies and pinching our backs. She would then roll us over and pinch our tummies. I know now that this was some kind of energy treatment she was giving us.

She would often say someone's name and the phone would ring and it would be that person. She would also say things like, "When is my little brother coming, Momma?" Or, "I was your sister once, but now you're my Mommy."

Her Dad and I know how special she is and how important it is for us to bring her up much differently then the ways we were brought up. Some days we don't know what we are doing, we just do what feels right and make the rest up as we go along. We hope we can help her achieve her life's purpose and be happy, things that all parents want of their children.

End Crystal Mom and Daughter Story

The difference between Indigos and Crystals lies in their vibrational energies and their auras – Crystals have an even higher frequency than Indigos and their auras contain unique colors never experienced before, or at least not that we have ever been aware of. These children have strong emotional and spiritual needs and their high vibrations make it difficult for them to participate in the world as it exists. When things get too tough for them, they simply cannot cope and they retreat to the peace and safety of their own inner world.

Our school systems, social structures, families, and ways of life have followed patterns that have not changed for many generations. And yet, they no longer serve our needs. These children will make it very clear to us where we need to make changes and what needs to happen next. It is important not to be afraid of these changes and know that they are for our greater good.

One aspect of the Crystal energy is that Crystal children require a great deal of physical attention, which involves being held and touched in loving and nurturing ways. Crystals are so loving and gentle and they need a lot of love from their parents, families and care givers. Their needs include a great deal of physical contact that is more than just touching and holding. There is a strong energy exchange with physical contact and from that they get the reassurance they need to know that they are here at the right time, there is love for them, and they will be safe. This will help meet the Crystal children's needs so that they can be prepared for their journey when it is time for them to begin their work here to teach us the ways of love and peace.

Around 2000, the first true Crystal children began to incarnate. This was because, as mentioned earlier, the new energy grid on the planet could now support these clear and powerful beings who have a higher vibrational frequency. Each Crystal child that is born is born on the new energy grid, and has the potential to be a fully awakened and conscious master at the level of the Christ Consciousness. Crystal children are spiritual masters in their own right.

The Crystal children are beautiful. They generally have large clear eyes that seem to look into your soul because, in fact, that is what they are doing. They are often calm and focused, but they can become hyperactive when their energy is out of alignment. They are very loving and nurturing and enjoy sharing their energies with others who might have need of them. They are powerful, and often have no fear at all. They can be very sensitive to food and to the environment as they are born with the clear systems needed on the new energy grid.

They are clairvoyant and psychic. They see angels and spirit guides, and can often feel and see the future. They know about past lives, and can often talk about who they were in past lives.

They are also very connected as a group, and much of their work for the planet is done on the levels of higher consciousness as a group. This is one reason Crystal children are sometimes tired and irritable and grumpy. They have often been working very hard on the higher energy levels to help the shift.

The Crystal children are moving into our hearts and upgrading our energy systems. The Crystals are helping us to claim our power and open our hearts, and to anchor ourselves firmly in the new energy grid. They are teaching us to accept our spiritual gifts as our birthright, and to see the creation of miracles as a normal activity. They are teaching us to honor our planet and ourselves and to see the beauty and the wonder and the joy of all creation.

We are learning to live as they do, in the present moment, not influenced by past or future. We are learning to live from the heart, to forgive and exercise tolerance and unconditional acceptance.

Chapter 3

Rainbow Children

*Think of yourself as an incandescent power, illuminated and
perhaps forever talked to by God and his
messangers…Brenda Ueland*

The Rainbow children are the third generation of special children
that have come to help humanity evolve. Different from the
Indigo and Crystal children, Rainbow children have a few more
interesting characteristics. The Rainbow children are generally
born in the year 2000 and above. In some cases, there might also
be a few scouts that came to earth before 2000. The few Rainbow
children that are here today are born from early Crystal scouts that
were born earlier.

As the name implies, the Rainbow children come to earth with a
few more other spectrum of ray color. They are born on the ninth
dimension of consciousness, the dimension of collective
consciousness.

As many people might have experienced, the Rainbow children
bring joy and harmony to their families. Unlike the Indigo and
Crystal children, the Rainbow child is born to smile, which is
accompanied by their huge hearts that are full of forgiveness.

The Rainbow child generally recovers from the state of negative
emotion quickly. This is also an important key that they hold,
emotional mastery. Rainbow children are psychic and have the
ability to read people's feelings. This gift is usually revealed as
they grow older.

Rainbow Children are psychic. Beyond this and perhaps more so, they have strong wills and strong personalities. Their gifts do not stop there. They are known to be natural healers and instant manifesters. It is said that whatever they need or desire, they can instantly manifest.

As would be expected, they have a connection to color. In fact, they resonate with the colors around them. They are drawn to color: colorful surroundings and brightly colored clothes. Their energy is expressed in other ways too, as they are high-energy children. Their enthusiasm is demonstrated in their creativity. The Rainbow children are thought to be the builders of the New World, using Divine will.

Doreen Virtue describes characteristics of Rainbow children:
- Very few currently incarnated.
- Parents are crystal adults.
- Have never incarnated before.
- Have no karma.
- Do not choose dysfunctional families.
- They are all about service.
- May have big eyes like the crystal children, but they are totally trusting.
- Entirely fearless of everybody.
- Bringing in the healing rainbow energy previously brought through Reiki, QiGong, and Pranic healing and other hands on healing.

Crystal children can also be very high energy, have strong personalities, be creative, and can instantly manifest anything they want or need.

At a young age, the Rainbow children are able to express their needs and wants. These children actually own a great deal of personal power. Rainbow children may be misinterpreted as stubborn. However, that is our misconception. Rainbow children are born with knowledge on proper character integration. This will develop depending on their parents because the character integration will change if there is negative programming given to the child. As a Rainbow parent, the idea is to recognize what positive traits your Rainbow child holds.

Rainbow children will also have immunity against junk food. Most Rainbow children are able to handle mutated cells and food products, which may result in poisoning. This is considered a very important ability, as most people may not recognize the toxins contained in junk food, and the Rainbow child can take and process these types of foods with no problem. This is because of the blood that the Rainbow child carries which has the ability to cleanse the toxins and unwanted bacteria in the food and air. So a Rainbow child may have a lot of physical clearing in the beginning stages of life. This will change once they grow older and learn how to clear ethereally or spiritually.

Astonishingly, the Rainbow children come with no karma. Rainbow children will enjoy the life on earth learning with absolutely no strings attached to their past. This is because they do not really continue from any previous cycle of reincarnation. This is also why they have a very high-energy frequency and physical energy.

The rainbow child is very hyperactive. They can run the whole night and really tire you out. This is a problem that parents of Rainbow children might face.

The purpose of the Rainbow children is to complete the final stages of the foundation that the Indigo and Crystal children have made. The three children, Indigo, Crystal, and Rainbow each have a specific task. The Indigo children are to break down the paradigm of traditional thinking. Then the Crystal children will build their foundation on the broken paradigm. Finally, the Rainbow children are here to build on to what the Indigo and Crystal children began.

Few writers have written on the Rainbow children because of their current status as toddlers. However, it is important to know that these children will play an important role in the earth's evolution.

Parents of Rainbow children should understand that their children are special and parents should appreciate the gifts they have. These gifts will help you evolve as they evolve with you.

The Rainbow children are just starting to show up on this planet, although there are already some scouts around. More Rainbow children will arrive as children of the Crystal scouts and also when humanity raises its vibrational frequency, universal consciousness, and the concept of oneness.

Doreen Virtue says, "The Rainbow children are perfectly balanced in their male and female energies. They are confident without aggressiveness; they are intuitive and psychic without effort; they are magical and can bend time, become invisible, and go without sleep and food. The Crystal children's sensitivities make them vulnerable to allergies and rashes. The angels say that the Rainbow children will have overcome this aspect… Rainbow children have no karma, so they have no need to choose chaotic childhoods for spiritual growth…The Rainbow children operate purely out of joy, and not out of need or impulse. The babies will be recognized, because their energy is one of giving to parents, and not of neediness. Parents will realize that they cannot out-give their Rainbow children, for these children are a mirror of all actions and energy of love. Whatever loving thoughts, feelings, and actions that you send to them are magnified and returned a hundred-fold."

A Message from Celia Fenn on the Rainbow Children
This message was received on the Venus Transit (8th June 2004) via Daniel Barnard:

Dearest human brothers and sisters, we bring you this message of joy and power at this time, because we are now bringing a powerful new energy to the planet. It is the power of the HEART, and as Venus transits your sun, the male and female energies blend into a prism of Rainbow light, and we, the Rainbow children, begin to radiate our power into the collective consciousness.

Our message is simple - but it requires of you, our elder brothers and sisters, to make a deep shift in your way of thinking, feeling, and living. We want you to realize that we, the Star children, have been coming to your planet in waves of incarnation since the 1970s. We have been coming to show you how you have shifted and how you need to return to balance so that your planet can return to balance.

The Indigo children showed you how rigid and inflexible and destructive you had become. The Crystals showed you how closed and unfeeling you had become, and we, the Rainbow children, are here to teach you how to open your hearts and truly feel the Great Heart that beats at the center of the Universe. With each radiant pulse, the Universe shimmers with the energies of the Divine Father/Mother and each of you receives these waves of Gold and Silver light. These waves of radiant energy are the keys to opening your heart to the truth of who and where you are.
End A Message from Celia Fenn on Rainbow Children

A Message from a Rainbow Parent (Eri Morningstar)
My daughter, who is two, is very much a Rainbow child. The word passionate does not even begin to describe her personality. She enters the world every day with a powerful energy, exerting her will, creativity, and energy into everything she does. While her older Crystal brother is laid back and patient, she is charging

forward with her voice on extra loud volume, doing this, doing that, she hardly ever stops to sit down for a moment or two! She even eats on the run, taking little bites here and there in between jumping on the trampoline or running by with a doll stroller at full speed.

She LOVES clothes and COLOR, and will spend a lot of time changing clothes every day, and her clothes have to be clean and neat, or she removes them and chooses new ones, throwing the soiled ones at me and exclaiming loudly, "Wash them, mama, thank you!" She will also spend a lot of time picking through the crayons, and selecting every hue of her favorite colors: pink and purple and then drawing with those hues.

She seems very sensitive and attuned to color for a two-year old. She even describes things in her life by what color they are as in pink sparkle shoes, pretty purple shirt, my yellow cup, baby's blue cup and so on. She names colors all day long and if she discovers a new color she does not know a name for, like a hue of another color, she will ask me, "What's this?" and I better answer RIGHT AWAY, because if I am on the phone or at the computer and do not immediately stop what I am doing to address her needs, she will shake my arm and her voice will repeat, "What's this, What's THIS, WHHHATTTTS TTTTHHHIIISSS?!!!!!!!!!!!!!!!" Until I answer. Then she says quietly, "Oh" and runs off to play with her new color discovery.

We have not seen the same psychic abilities as her older brother, but she has her own gifts. Healing seems to be one of them. She is very aware of other peoples "owies" and is always ready to kiss them to make them better.

Her strong will and passionate creativity make her very fun to watch as she scampers about. She will create elaborate costumes out of feather boas and velvet fabrics and talk or hum to herself as she acts out her little world. She is a true joy to be around most of the time, as long as I make sure she gets my full attention if she needs something because patience does not seem to be a very big Rainbow child quality.

End A Message from a Rainbow Parent

Rainbow children are already attuned to the world we are moving towards when things will instantly manifest. Humanity as a whole is not there yet, so the mass consciousness grid holds back instant manifestation from being commonplace. A toddler has a hard time understanding that. They feel if they "think" juice, well then juice ought to naturally appear instantly. In higher dimensions this may be true and it will be true here on Earth as well, thanks to the Rainbow kids making it so.

Rainbow Children tend to:
- Have very strong wills and personalities.
- Be very high energy.
- Be very attuned to color and color vibrations around them.
- Have passionate creativity.
- Love bright clothing and colorful environments.
- Bubble over with enthusiasm for everything in life.
- Expect instant manifestation of whatever they think/need.
- Have healing abilities.
- Have telepathy.
- Recover from negative emotion quickly.
- Have an uncanny ability to read people's feelings.

The Rainbow children seem to be here to implement the Divine Will and they will use their strong will and energy to build the New World on the foundation of peace and harmony the Crystal children are laying down. The Crystal children are only able to lay down that foundation because the Indigo children have already forged the path and have broken down all of the old barriers. They are all-important and have to come in this sequence to accomplish their goals.

Rainbows are highly sensitive, loving, forgiving, and magical like the Crystal children. The difference is that the Rainbows have never before been on earth, so they have no karma to balance. The Rainbows, therefore, choose entirely peaceful and functional households. They don't need chaos or challenges to balance karma or grow.

As the other Crystal children grow older, they will be the peace-loving parents who birth the new Rainbow children. The Rainbows being born right now are the scouts, and the large influx of Rainbows will occur during the years 2010 through 2030.

Rainbow children are absolutely open hearted, love unconditionally, and have no fear towards any stranger. Unlike the Crystal children who only display affection to people warranting their trust, the Rainbows are universally affectionate. They heal us with their huge heart chakras, and envelop us in a blanket of rainbow-colored energy that we so sorely need. They are our earth angels.

Chapter 4

Indigo to Crystal to Rainbow Transitions

Energy is the essence of life…Oprah Winfrey

As our Star children raise their vibrational frequencies, they will experience a shift into a multi-dimensional awareness, energy, or a shift in consciousness. In fact, this can happen in people who have been on a spiritual path and are able to handle this type of energy shift.

Celia Fenn has written about symptoms that may occur during a vibrational shift, which may include:

1.   Sudden extreme sensitivity to people and environments. A person who has previously been sociable and active suddenly finds they can't bear to be in shopping malls or in crowded environments such as restaurants.
2.   An increase in psychic ability and awareness. This most often manifests in the ability to almost hear the inner thoughts and feelings of others. This can be disconcerting if the person imagines that everyone else can also read his or her thoughts and feelings. Also, an extreme sensitivity to negative energy in certain environments or people, including the inability to tolerate someone who had previously been close.
3.   This increased sensitivity can lead to panic attacks or anxiety attacks. These can occur at any time, even when the person wakes up at night. Often there is no valid reason for the attack, although the person will often seek to find a reason.

4.   People might also find themselves zoning out for long periods of time, just wanting to sit and do nothing. This can be irritating to someone who has previously been very energetic and active. This is just the consciousness adjusting to spending more time in the higher dimensions and less time in the 3rd and 4th dimensions. Related to this is the need to rest and sleep for far longer than usual and a general slowing down.

5.   Obsessive anxieties about humans being destroyed (by pollution, lack of resources, aliens, technology, etc). This is because multi-dimensional consciousness can access all levels of the group mind, including that part which holds the fears and anxieties about the survival of the species. Since the person is often concerned about their own survival, they tend to resonate with this part of the group mind or morphogenetic field.

6.   An obsessive need to understand what is happening, leading to the mind becoming overactive and the person fearing they are losing it or suffering from burn-out. Also, a fear of going mad and being unable to cope with everyday life in the future. Psychologists and doctors seem able to offer very little help.

7.   Depression for no reason, or related to the crisis state. This is often just the consciousness clearing out old layers of energy that need to be released. It is not necessary to process or relive the experience, just allow the body to release the energy. Have patience with the process and know that it will pass.

8.   Disrupted sleep patterns, often waking up to three times a night, or just at about 3 a.m. Again, this is just the consciousness adapting to new cycles of activity. Higher consciousness is often more active at night since the lower dimensions are quiet at this time.

9.   Feeling strange electrical energy waves through the body. The Crystal body is incredibly sensitive and feels solar and lunar waves, cosmic waves, and energies from the galactic center. Often these energies are assisting in the process of rewiring the body to carry higher energies. Speaking from experience, I know how uncomfortable this can be. But the body eventually

acclimates to dealing with these energy waves. You will probably find them to be more intense around a full moon. The best way I have found of dealing with this phenomenon is to go outside and stand barefoot on the ground and imagine the energy running through your body and into the earth.

10. A whole range of physical sensations and experiences usually related to detoxification. The Crystal body holds no toxins, but allows everything to pass through it. In fact, the eventual trick to being Crystal is just to allow everything to pass through and hold on to nothing. This is the ultimate state of detachment. At this stage, the body needs to release years of toxic waste, whether physical, emotional, or mental. The release is always through the physical body, which presents symptoms such as intense fatigue, muscle and joint pains, especially in the hips and knees; headaches, especially at the base of the skull; and neck and shoulder pains.

11. Dizziness and spaciness. This is because you are in higher states of consciousness. You need to get used to being at these levels and staying grounded at the same time. These sensations tend to increase with solar flares and full moons as well.

12. Increased appetite and putting on weight. This is because the body needs huge amounts of energy to power this process.

13. The ability to see beyond the veils. That is, to become aware of spirits, devas, ETs, and angels as a reality and to communicate with them. This can be very frightening if the person is not accustomed to this kind of other dimensional awareness.

The purpose of the Indigo to Crystal to Rainbow transition is ascension. We are all ascending to a higher dimension of consciousness and a higher vibrational frequency. This spiritual evolution is often referred to as ascension, or consciously elevating the vibratory rate of our physical and other energetic bodies to the Christ level.

Ascension is about realizing our God and Goddess selves and creating Heaven on earth. It is about embracing who we really are and dispelling the thought that we are separate from our Creator or the Divine. Ascension is also about bringing the higher and lower aspects of our being into complete harmony and alignment with our higher self or higher purpose in life. Everything in life that isn't in alignment with our higher purpose will just fall away with this process. There can be a difficult period of adjustment during the process of ascension and some of the adjustments can be hard to view as positive circumstances. This may mean ending relationships, moving, changing jobs, and further changes that may seem unsettling. However, it is necessary for these old patterns to fall away to make room for the new higher energy.

The ultimate goal in spiritual ascension is to align with a higher source and keep vibrational frequencies at a higher level to help you live out your life's purpose and find the special gifts and talents that you have to offer.

During the process of ascension, you may feel physically exhausted. You might even feel the need to sleep very long hours. Your physical bodies are aligning with the higher vibratory rate of your spiritual bodies to help facilitate the more complete alignment of both your higher and lower selves.

The mental effects of ascension may not be long lasting, but they do cause change in our mental state. You can also experience sadness and depression, which are feelings that can be part of the alignment process. As you become more centered within the peace and stillness of your soul and divine essence in the alignment process, the world around you may appear more frantic and chaotic for a time.

During ascension, you may also experience feelings of emptiness and loneliness, which is part of the complete surrender to the higher self. You will have released the hold of the lower-ego-self and will therefore have surrendered to the guidance of the higher-ego-self. These are two levels of the spirit where the lower-ego-self contains the potentials of ego and the higher-ego-self contains potentials of the soul.

Once the alignment is complete, you will experience deep feelings of peace and gratitude. Those of you who have completed your alignments will shine like a bright star and people around you will be able to feel and sense the light that now radiates from within. You will be a part of the changes that are occurring here on earth and you will help to transform the planet and create heaven on earth.

In order to ascend to a place of higher dimensional consciousness, you must become fully conscious. This means stopping old patterns and habits that prevent you from living in heightened awareness. This knowledge will bring you into the light of higher conscious awareness. There are many means for bringing limited aspects of self into the light of higher awareness and angels are tirelessly working on this to help you.

Ascension into higher dimensional consciousness can be done in many ways. Prayer, meditation, reading, and practicing good karma are all ways to help ascend to a higher vibrational frequency.

Gratitude is the fastest way to raise your vibrational frequency. Saying thank you and being grateful will help you ascend to higher dimensions of consciousness.

Living your life's purpose is another way to ascend. People often ask, "What is my life's purpose?" Your life's purpose can be learned by communication with your guides and angels. By raising vibrational frequencies to a higher level, it becomes easier to communicate with your higher self, your guides, and your angels who are here loving you and helping you to reveal your life's purpose.

For most lightworkers here on earth, it can take up to half their lifetimes to "wake up" to the fact that they have a mission here to help this earth. The feeling of "something is coming" or an idea of a "big mission" is quite common among lightworkers, which include Star children.

What is a big mission? A big mission is some significant event that every soul plans for to happen in their life that has a major impact on humanity or the earth in some way, either negative or positive depending on the soul's level and power. The big mission can be any one of an infinite number of things, but it is different for every soul, and in some way it makes a huge and lasting impact in the world that is not always realized at the moment it happens.

For example, for some souls, the "big mission" might be missionary work for a period of time, healing work, or that time they talked a teenager out of committing suicide, perhaps without even knowing it. Light workers, souls who are aware, and Star children, are awakened and conscious of their spiritual power and light. They are sensing the emerging quickening of time and energy in this three-dimensional world. The feelings of wanting or needing to begin their mission or purpose here on earth are becoming stronger with their ascension.

Ascension also brings about the expansion of the auric field and the chakras. This can be very tiring for Star children and other light workers. It is common for those that are ascending to need as much as nine to twelve hours of sleep a night.

Physics tells us that every thing is composed of energy. Even if we can't see it, energy exists at various frequencies, and is in essence, all things. Our bodies are essential in maintaining the harmony between our physical body and our soul. Ascension has ramifications for us on this physical world of mind and body. We see that there is a connection with the soul itself. Beyond this, it may help us on our spiritual perfection.

Parents of today are setting the foundation for raising ascending Star children. Parents are clearing their own negative energy and old emotions to help their children with their own ascension. The old ways, or the teaching and parenting skills that are on the old energy grid will begin to slowly change in the years to come. If people do not raise their vibrational frequencies to keep up with the ascending Star children and other light workers, they will not be able to handle the new higher frequencies here on earth and will become ill.

Ascension will allow Star children to be treated as the unique souls that they are. This new energy transition is being born through our children. Each year more and more Star children are coming into this world, affecting whole communities by their energy and their auric fields. We are all ascending whether we realize it or not.

Ascension will make it possible for all life to blossom and for all people to manifest their dreams, live their life's purpose, and experience the life intended for all souls. In time, through ascension, unity will allow all life to stand with compassion, love, respect, and a value of wholeness and oneness.

Chapter 5

Environmental Stress and Your Star Child

I just realized that there is going to be a lot of painful times in life, so I better learn to deal with it right away...Trey Parker and Matt Stone

Stress is a response to any situation or factor that creates a negative emotional or physical change or combination of both emotional and physical changes. Stress is an unavoidable aspect of life. People of all ages can experience stress. Some stress is helpful because it provides motivation. However, excessive stress can interfere with life, activities, health, and energy.

Star children are far more open and sensitive than most other people to stress. Their hearing, senses, and vision are more acute. This will become more commonplace as the energy shift continues on the earth because they know psychically what is in your mind and heart and mirror your emotions causing additional stress.

Indigo, Crystal, and Rainbow children are distressed by loud noises, crowds, television sets, and people with bad energy. Their response to these outside noises will be to withdraw and become depressed or they may become hyperactive and destructive. It is important to minimize noise and stress in your child's life.

Try to let your Star child play outside as much as possible in a natural environment as it is very important that they stay connected to nature. Limit television, computer games, and cartoons. Encourage your child's imagination by reading books, coloring, and creating fun games. This quiet and tranquil home environment will positively affect the behavior of your child.

There have been many studies on the effects of too much television and video games on children's behavior. Star children are different. They are mirrors and what goes on in their environment will be magnified and reflected back to the universe. Your Star child can read your energy, thoughts, and heart. They understand exactly what you're thinking and feeling even if it remains unstated.

It is also crucial that parents try to create and keep a harmonious home for themselves and their children. Star children are deeply affected by the energy of people around them. Parents need to realize that a child's home needs to be a sanctuary, a place for their spiritual growth and encouragement to reach their life's purpose.

Children are exposed to all kind of stress and traumatic experiences of today's world. They are aware of terrorism, kidnappings, obesity, epidemics, bullying, teen suicide, and so many other horrific events.

There are also huge amounts of pressure placed on children by achievement-oriented parents to excel at home, school, sports, music and extracurricular activity, while dealing with the stresses of home and school. What is this all for? Our goals should be to raise and nurture our children to help them develop and reach their spiritual goals – their purpose in life. If we can add in environmental consciousness, fearlessness, and show them the world is all one, we will have added a bonus to their upbringing.

It is not surprising that teen depression, suicide, obesity, ADD, and ADHD are a national epidemic. Other disorders are rising, including sleeping disorders, stomach problems, headaches, migraines, and asthma.

Stress contributes to many health issues in our children. Stress can be caused by anything from hearing their parents' fight to going to school and finding a substitute teacher for the day. All children are unique and sensitive in their own ways.

Ask yourself, as a parent, "How different would my children's lives be if they knew how to slow down their pace, relax and meditate, and see life more clearly?" How would you feel if you were to watch your child relax and enjoy life? How would you feel if you could watch their self-esteem grow? These are all things that we would love to see in our children.

Read your child books and show them how to manage their own energy, stress, and anxiety. Meditating, yoga, and other healthy activities will help your children create their own healthy and peaceful lives.

Guided Grounding Meditation
Guided meditations are a wonderful way to calm the minds of children. It is wonderful to allow children to find their own inner silence and truth, which helps them to relax, unwind, and to live a life full of possibilities that they can creat for themselves.

Find a quiet, comfortable spot. Make sure the lighting is soft and play soft meditation music if you wish. Remind your child to breathe during this meditation.

Lay quietly and comfortably and breathe in. When you do, picture a beautiful white light coming down through the top of your head and out through the bottom of your feet. On the out breath, breathe deep and let out all the bad air, the worry, and fear of the day. Let the bottoms of your feet connect deep down into Mother Earth. You are grounded. White light shines down over your body from above while your feet are rooted to the center of the earth. You are here. You are safe. You are loved. It is ok to let go and know that you will be taken care of by your angels and guides. All is as it should be and unfolding in the Divine timing of the universe.

Walk down a mountainous path. The stone walls are tall and loom around you. The energy of angels and guides live here. Their love and strength fills your spirit with joy. It is a mysterious place full of wonder and light. You look up to see white light shining over you and you feel showered in their love.

Sit down at your computer and look at the screen. The angels and guides have an important message for you. What do you see on the screen? What does it say? Is there something written or a story being played out? Is there sound?

Continue walking and listen to the sound of water running. Follow the sounds of the water along the mountainous path as you walk. You are curious and eager to see what is up ahead. The path before you turns gently into curved steps leading towards a garden. Walking gingerly along the path, you see a pool of water toward your left and a stream of trickling water coming from the rocks above that gently drops into its reflective surface.

You approach the water. What do you do? Do you look into it? Do you reach towards it? Drink from it? Dive into it?

There is an angel or guide who wishes to greet you on the path. Who is this person? Is he/she in the water or beside it? Ask for a name. Ask if there is a message.

You sit on the bank of the pool and reflect upon the feeling of this place. What do you feel? What do you see?

Your time has come to leave. The ones who have been with you bid you farewell and send you messages of love. You travel back up the stone stairs. You climb up into the sunshine and feel the air on your face, the world right in its place. You now have a clear vision of what is to come. You feel safe and loved.

White light shines down on you and your feet are rooted to the center of the earth.

When you are ready, bring yourself back to the sounds of your room. Feel your arms, your shoulders, your legs, and your feet. Wiggle your fingers and your toes and when you are ready, open your eyes and remember your experience.
End Guided Grounding Meditation

Most children feel stress long before they grow up. Many children have to cope with family conflicts, changes in school, childcare arrangements, divorce, and sometimes violence in their homes. In addition to this, your Star child is hypersensitive and knows what is going on in your head and heart, even the unspoken words, feelings, and emotions.

It isn't always obvious when a child is stressed. Some children may say, "My stomach hurts," rather than stating they feel overwhelmed by something.

There are many things a parent can do to help relieve stress in their Star child:
1. Parents can help their children learn to keep the harmful effects of stress to a minimum.

2. Parents should monitor stress in their own lives and remember that parental fighting is very unsettling for children, especially Star children.

3. Keep communication lines open at all times. Children feel so much better about themselves and their lives if they have a good relationship with their parents, family, and loved ones.

4. Make sure your children have plenty of time to play with other kids, especially outside in nature. Encourage friendships and other fun activities.

5. Make sure you keep a routine and limit over stimulation. Your children should have plenty of sleep, exercise, and healthy food on a daily basis.

6. Tell your children you love them everyday. Be sure to show them how much you love them as well.

7. Limit activities. For example, suggest your child play only one sport. Help work on your Star child's life purpose rather than being a goal-oriented parent.

8. Spend plenty of time together as a family. Do fun things together. Have a good time and be unproductive instead of just doing chores.

9. Trust yourself and your instincts as a parent. You know your children better than anyone else does, so take a good hard look. Be honest with yourself about what you see.

It is important that Star children talk about their problems with their parents. Parents also need to understand that these new children will be picking up on their emotions. It is important for parents, as well as Star children, to be open to solving stressful issues in their lives.

Most parents want to create a perfect world for their children and they want to protect them. Let your children make themselves happy, don't do it for them or try to protect them. They will learn good life skills by learning how to calm themselves down and learn how to play and grow their imagination about the world around them.

Staying Spiritually Grounded

Staying spiritually grounded or serving humanity from the spirit is a good way to relieve emotional and environmental stress. This means attending to your inner spirituality. As Star children grow spiritually, the level of consciousness and vibrational frequency will also grow.

Grounding is a good way to rise above the level of ego to an elevated platform and look around and within to see what is really needed in our lives.

Star children must find a way that is specific to them to keep their feet on the ground and remember who they are and why they are here, in order to deal with the effects of environmental stress.

Getting these children outside and back to nature is always a good start in keeping them spiritually grounded.

End Staying Spiritually Grounded

Energy from emotional and physical stress can spread into your immediate environment, including your home. Your home is a sanctuary where you can relax and unwind.

Your body is the home of your spirit. It is a sacred temple to house the Divine. Your house is the home of your sacred body, the temple of your soul, and so is an extension of your spirit's sacred space. Everything you do in your home is reflected in your body. Everything within your body, heart, and spirit can be seen in your home and in your life.

If you want to see changes in your life and help relieve stress, you can change your home. If you want to see changes in your heart, your love life, and your attitude, making small changes in your home can help. You must create space for your spirit to dwell, both in your heart and in your home in peace and harmony.

De-cluttering your home by using Feng Shui, soft lighting, music, or aromatherapy are all ways to help improve your home and make it your haven. Another good technique is to enter your home and walk around as if you were seeing it for the first time as an Angel. What do you see that is ugly, makes you feel sad, upset, tired, or frustrated? What do you see that is beautiful, that brings you joy, and reminds you of love?

Take a few moments in each room of your house, looking around, opening your closets, and looking in your drawers and cabinets. Where is it that you cringe when you enter or open it? Make a few notes, jotting down any observations of feelings or emotions that come up, any negative feelings, and likewise any positive feelings, anything that feels really good in your home and enlightens your heart and spirit when you see it.

There are many ways to help manage stress for parents and Star children. Find what works best for your children and your family and also trust in the abilities of your Star children to help find the best way in managing and alleviating stress.

Chapter 6
Knowing Ways

Apparently there is nothing that cannot happen today...Mark Twain

Today's Indigo, Crystal, and Rainbow children share a very unique characteristic, they are all about seeing the truth. Not simple truths, like the sky is blue, the sun is warm, and rain is wet, but very complex truths that include spiritual understanding and a sense of purpose that many parents never had as children. These children are uncomfortable with untruths and outright lies. They are willing to stand up to them, to argue against them, and to defend their position without backing down.

The Indigo, Crystal, and Rainbow children are not willing to accept things at face value because they need to know why things are the way they are. They do not accept distortions of the truth from their parents in any way. They simply do not understand why we do not tell the truth. Furthermore, they will insist that we do, no matter how painful it is for us to do so. Star children would rather know the truth than deal with untruth. If we are not willing to deal with them on this level, they will pester and hound us until we do.

Their insistence on knowing the truth is not just about uncovering deception, no matter how well intentioned it is. Their truth is actually a need for sincerity, to live in harmony with their spirit, their connection, and their entire being. Anything that is not in alignment with this truth or knowing puts them out of balance and they cannot simply disregard it, as past generations of children once did. They must put things straight, get things right, and uncover the truth. This need for sincerity extends to what is going on in the world around them in their communities, their cities, their countries, and the world in general.

Star children do not accept our willingness to tolerate discrimination based on color or gender. Star children appear to be oblivious to differences in color and culture. To them, a black person and a white person are exactly the same, as is someone from Asia or someone from South America. More and more Star children are involved in interracial and intercultural relationships than any other generation. They are also intolerant of society's criticisms of their choices. As far as they're concerned, there is no difference between them and anyone else. They may ask us to explain what we are talking about when we mention differences in people.

Today, humanity is much more accepting of its spirituality. Star children have grown up with the ability to connect with others on a global basis and this has given rise to their opinions about the oneness of humanity. They do not understand why we cannot do the same. For them, there is one truth: that we are all the same and deserve the same things.

Many children held bake sales, sold their toys, and did what they could for the tsunami victims in South and Southeast Asian in 2004. It was their way of showing the world that they connected with these people and were willing to show compassion and do what they could to help them. This is also an example of the truth and knowing that they hold. Why should some of the world's people suffer when others do not and we should all help each other.

Crystal children are born with an incredible knowing. They can access the sixth dimension of consciousness, which is the realm of the Christened Child or Magical Child, with the potential to open up to the ninth dimension of consciousness. All Crystal children are born onto this level of awareness. They have immediate access to the magical and spiritual aspects of who they are and are able to blend imagination and creation in amazing ways.

Maddy's Story
My daughter had been playing with a bird feather we found. One morning we lost the feather. My daughter said, "Mommy, I want another feather, I want TWO feathers."

I promised after her nap that day that we would go look for another feather. When my daughter and I walked down our stairs that afternoon there were two feathers directly at the bottom of our stairs. These were the only feathers we have ever found in our yard in two years.

I have known that my daughter was a Crystal child. Watching her instantly manifest small things in her world is amazing to watch.
End Maddy's Story

If Crystal children were left alone, they would create a magical planet for us. Unfortunately, they have to deal with third dimensional consciousness and they struggle with the patterns and behaviors they find here.

There are many ways Star children and people in general receive psychic information. This may include clairvoyance, which is the ability to receive psychic information by seeing it with one's mind in mental pictures. Another might be clairaudience, which occurs by hearing the information. There is also clairsentience, which is picking up information through feeling, smelling, tasting, or sensing someone else's energy. Information may also be received from angels, guides, spirit guides, or maybe even

61

loved ones that have passed away. A knowing is another way to receive information. A "knowing" is receiving a lump of information with immediate and complete understanding.

Whatever method Star children receive information, it is important that this information that comes in through the third eye not be feared. This information will keep these special children protected by giving them the ability to ferret out lies and deception and it will help change the energy on our planet.

Author's Story

When I was in the 3rd grade, we moved into a house in the foothills of Albuquerque, New Mexico. My first memories of seeing ghosts occurred in this house. The house we moved into was newly built. However, I "knew" the bricks around our fireplace came from another structure and were reused in our house.

Shortly after moving in, I began seeing an old-fashioned cowboy ghost. He had a cowboy hat, bandana around his neck, bullets in a belt across his chest, a gun on each side of his hips hung low around his waist, and spurs on his boots.

This may seem quite enchanting, but I assure you, it was anything but. This cowboy ghost came to our house with the bricks. Somehow his energy was transferred with these bricks. As an eight-year-old, I knew this information – it was a knowing – information that just came to me in one lump sum.

On a regular basis, this ghost would visit me. These visits were terrifying. He would often step up on my beanbag or desk in a threatening manner with intent to shoot me as if he were ready for one of those old fashioned shoot-outs. He would also walk up and down our hallway with his spurs clinging and clanging as he walked. These hallway walks happened on a regular basis.

The ghost knew that I could see and hear him. I would tell my parents and brothers over and over about the ghost and what he did, but they would all smile at me and tell me I was dreaming. Eventually, my mother would yell at me to shut up when I mentioned it.

Not long after we moved into that house my family started fighting on a regular basis. I remember my dad and oldest brother having a very physical fight one morning, rolling on the floor hitting each other like they were in a bar room brawl. I believe my cowboy ghost caused and fed off this bad energy in our home. At eight years old, I knew this and I was confused that no other family members felt or knew what was happening, or the reason for it.

I know now all about this entity that caused bad energy in our home. The damage caused by this bad energy was never repaired for some members of my family. I would like to think that if my family had listened to me even though I was very young, we could have moved or cleared the ghost out of the house.

When I look back to my elementary school days, I remember seeing, hearing, and knowing things that others did not. The worst part was that nobody would believe or listen to me.

I spent many, many years feeling frightened and alone because of these experiences. As I grew older, I finally understood about energy, psychic visions, guides, and angels and the purpose of all of these things.

In this book, I say over and over to help your Star children figure out what their life's purpose is and how they will contribute to humanity as a whole. You must also help these special children understand and be unafraid of their gifts. I believe the energy has changed enough that most people will understand that these experiences are real and we're not alone.

My heart sings with joy that perhaps by writing this book, I can help take the fear out of these experiences for others. I know there are no accidents. My early ghostly experiences and other situations growing up made me strong and able to write about it and share my story with others to help them understand and be strong as well.

I can promise you with every ounce of my "knowing" that no one is alone in this world. We all have angels and guides that are with us every minute of our lives and others that will come and go as our lessons are learned. Even for people who do not believe, their angels NEVER give up on them. There is no judgement, only love from your angels.
End Author's Story

The most wonderful aspect of Star children is their willingness to take on the world and learn to make their own way through it. Star children will get to the point where they are able to mold society into something that reflects their energies and values. The truth that they hold and defend so well will reflect their integrity and spirituality.

Chapter 7
The Importance of
Healthy Food

Beauty isn't something on the outside. It's your insides that count! You gotta eat green stuff to make sure you're pretty on the inside...Takayuki Ikkaku, Arisa Hosaka and Toshihiro Kawabata

Star children are sensitive to all vibrational input. This includes environmental pollutants and toxic food.

Food has energy, a vibrational frequency, and even an aura to it. When food is taken in the body, it affects your energy. Good energy is important in the process of ascension and eating healthy food is just another way in changing this energy.

The subtle energy field for all living things is called the aura. This life force energy is a multidimensional manifestation of luminous universal energy, which surrounds and permeates all living things.

For people, the aura contains the entire blue print for our life. It is our consciousness including all our thoughts, feelings, and awareness that originates from within the aura. The aura contains all of our life experiences from the moment we are born until the moment we die. It also contains all memory of past life information carried forward by karma.

The aura is a pulsating, multidimensional body of consciousness which reflects our true thoughts and feelings because it constantly responds to our internal reality. In fact, the state of the subtle bodies, auric layers, and the chakras can fluctuate from day to day in response to the impact of our experiences and how we process them. By observing the state of the aura, the colors and structure, we can obtain vital information regarding physical, emotional, mental, and spiritual well being.

Colors reflect the general well being of the aura. A healthy aura will glow with clear, luminous colors. Murky colors within the aura often indicate the presence of disease or illness. The location and extent of blocked, dysfunctional energy can reveal the stage and progression of an illness or disease. Colors can also reflect mental and emotional states.

The aura is comprised of individual and interrelated bodies of consciousness and layers of etheric energy. The four subtle bodies of consciousness that defines our personality, our perception, our direction in life, and our soul's expression are known as the etheric body, the emotional body, the mental body, and the spiritual body.

Every food has an aura even if it is unhealthy food because of the vitamins, minerals, amino acids, and enzymes in them that each emits their own specific vibrational color frequency.

The color of fruits and vegetables energize each of the chakras and affect the aura. For example, plums, blueberries, and purple grapes are examples of food that energize the crown, brow, and throat chakra.

Blue is the color of the heavens, the illusory, and the unreal. It is a cooling color, bringing peace, tranquility, and faith in oneself and others. Blue helps with communication and self-expression, and opens our minds to realities beyond the physical senses. It stimulates our appreciation of music and the arts and can help us break away from order and routine.

With its cooling properties, blue takes the heat out of inflammatory conditions, reduces fevers, and temperatures, and lowers blood pressure. It influences any disorders linked to the throat and respiratory system, such as sore throats, simple goiter, asthma, and overactive thyroid.

An individual with a well-balanced influence of blue in his or her aura will feel inspired, calm, and at peace with the world around them. A shortage of blue energy can cause an individual to withdraw from the world, and become frightened, timid, manipulative, and unreliable.

Green leafy vegetables such as broccoli, spinach, green beans, and spinach energize the heart chakra. Greens purify the blood and help the heart and blood circulation.

Green is the color of nature and renewal. It balances our energies and brings peace and harmony into our lives. The color of healing and of hope, green can give us stability and direction and awaken greater friendliness and faith.

A good balance of green in your color chart makes you feel content and satisfied with life. It fills you with optimism and confidence.

Greens sustain a strong faith in the notion of a mysterious, inexplicable force guiding all of nature. With green in your aura, you never fail to wonder at the power and beauty of the natural world and delight in even the tiniest flower. Your intuitive and artistic powers are at their height in the spring because of the intimate connection you feel to new life. It mediates between the worlds of spirit and matter. The spiritual goal of green is to raise physical and emotional energies from the solar plexus and heart chakras and transform emotions of fear into pure divine love expressed through the throat chakra.

Yellow squash, corn, and yellow peppers energize the solar plexus chakra. Oranges, yams, and pumpkin energize the naval chakra.

A powerful primary color, yellow links to logic and the intellect. It is a hot, expansive color that makes you feel happy and optimistic. It gives freedom to do and be what we like. It helps you surmount obstacles and get rid of emotional blockages that may be restricting personal development.

Yellow affects the nervous system and related illnesses, so if there is an excess of yellow in an aura, there may be times when rest and relaxation are needed. Skin conditions such as eczema and acne benefit from yellow, as it is an excellent purifier of the whole body and, by extension, the skin. It also influences the pancreas and diabetes. Its connection to the gall bladder and liver can be seen in the hallmark yellow color of jaundice. All the organs of the digestive system, including the stomach, duodenum and eliminative functions, are influenced by it. Yellow is particularly good for treating constipation and has even been known to trigger a change in insulin requirements.

Yellow links to the solar plexus chakra, which is central to our awareness of the self and power to be individual. It also celebrates our connection to the rest of humanity. The higher qualities of yellow are also to be found in the wisdom of gold, so the spiritual goal of yellow should be to harness and understand these powerful energies and use them to stimulate his or her awareness of the capacities and talents of other souls.

Red apples, beets, red grapes, and strawberries energize the root chakra.

Red is the color of physical energy, passion, and desire. A very powerful color, it is linked to our most primitive physical and emotional needs, particularly our will to survive.

The color red affects the circulatory system. Where your health is concerned, its influence can manifest itself in a variety of blood disorders such as anemia, high blood pressure, hot inflamed conditions, and an exaggerated amount of energy and drive. If you are lacking in energy, or suffering from physical exhaustion, introducing more red into your life will kick-start your system.

Chapter 8
Hearing and Seeing
is Believing

I can believe anything, provided that it is quite incredible...Oscar Wilde

Everyone is born with spiritual gifts, but most aren't aware that they have them or how to develop them. Angels and guides will try many times to reach you in your life in order to wake you up spiritually and help you complete your lessons you agreed upon before you were born.

Most children have invisible playmates which are actually angelic beings. Children seem to be more open younger in life and able to stay open and see their angels and guides. Often people will have dreams which are prophetic or illuminating. They may also have a sense of de ja vu when they feel they have dreamed of a situation or person that they have seen or have been in. Some people will feel the presence of a dead relative around them or see them after they have passed away. Many people will often know what someone is about to say or do, or pick up on someone else's thoughts. Some people can think of something they badly need and manifest it. These are all psychic gifts, gifts that we all have, but may have forgotten how to use.

Most people need to relearn how to use their psychic gifts. It is helpful if parents are supportive and believe in fostering these gifts. Most young children are psychic and see fairies, angels, guides, auras, and other planes of existence. Parents can shut their children down when they tell them that they are dreaming or to grow up.

Special Note
Often in life we say, "When you see it, you will believe it." Instead, we should say, "When I believe it, I will see it." Skeptics rarely have spiritual experiences because they don't have an open mind to explore this realm and don't allow themselves to believe what they can't hear or see.
End Special Note

It is important to recognize signs that are given to you by your angels and guides. For example, you may be thinking about becoming an accountant. Then you may run into a friend who is an accountant and tells you about the training he or she has had. Then you may walk past the bookstore that has a book about accounting in the window. Later that day or within a few days you may see a TV show on accounting. This is because your angels and guides are directing information to you concerning something that is spiritually important for you. Always look for coincidences in your life. There is no such thing as accidents, so keep your psychic antennae up and running.

Meditation and Psychic Development
Meditation is a good way to start spiritual and psychic development. When meditating, sit in a quite and relaxed place. It is important to calm the mind while meditating.

The first stage of meditation is to stop distractions and make the mind clearer and more lucid. This can be accomplished by practicing a simple breathing meditation. Choose a quiet place to meditate and sit in a comfortable position. Sit in the traditional cross-legged posture or in any other position that is comfortable for you. You can also sit in a chair if you prefer.

Sit with your eyes partially closed and turn your attention to your breathing. Breathe naturally, preferably through the nostrils, without attempting to control your breath, and try to become aware of the sensation of the breath as it enters and leaves the nostrils. This sensation is the object of meditation. Concentrate on it to the exclusion of everything else.

At first, your mind will be very busy, and you might even feel that the meditation is making it busier. In reality, you are just becoming more aware of how busy your mind actually is. There will be a great temptation to follow the different thoughts as they arise, but resist this and remain focused single-pointedly on the sensation of breathing. If you discover that your mind has wandered and is following your thoughts, immediately return it to the breathing. Repeat this as many times as necessary until your mind settles on the breathing.

If you practice patiently, gradually distracting thoughts will subside and you will experience a sense of inner peace and relaxation. You will feel lucid, spacious, and refreshed. When the incessant flow of distracting thoughts is calmed through concentration, the mind becomes unusually lucid and clear. Stay with this state of mental calm for a while.

Even though a breathing meditation is only a preliminary stage of meditation, it can be quite powerful. From this practice, it is possible to experience inner peace and contentment just by controlling the mind, without having to depend at all upon external conditions.

When the turbulence of distracting thoughts subsides and your mind becomes still, a deep happiness and contentment naturally arises from within. This feeling of contentment and well being helps to cope with the busyness and difficulties of daily life. So much of the stress and tension normally experienced comes from the mind, and many of the problems experienced, including ill health, are caused or aggravated by stress. Just by doing breathing meditation for ten or fifteen minutes each day, stress can be reduced. You will experience a calm, spacious feeling in the mind, and many problems will just seem to fall away. Difficult situations will become easier to deal with, you will naturally feel warm and well disposed towards other people, and your relationships with others will gradually improve.

Meditations can be prophetic, angelic, inspiring, illuminating or just peaceful. You never know quite what to expect.

Try to connect with nature while meditating. This is important because the sophisticated person living in a city may have lost contact with Mother Earth. Her energies empower us. Until we can see and feel the unity and feel grounded with the Earth, we are missing a valuable component to our spiritual development.
End Meditation and Psychic Development

During meditation, it is possible to connect with your angels and guides. Never be frightened or fearful when connecting with your angels and guides or others who have passed on to the spiritual plane. Spirits are generally loving beings. If you loved your Grandmother when she was alive and you weren't afraid of her then, why would you be afraid to see her as a loving spirit? Often, she will look the same, smile at you, and mentally send you a loving message. This is not frightening but reassuring. It proves she still exists on a nearby spiritual plane. These occurrences often happen spontaneously, when you least expect them and when you are in a relaxed state.

However, when you are consciously trying to first contact any spirits, it is important that you learn the techniques, particularly of personal protection, from an experienced medium, classes, or books. Just as there is polarity, or opposites in life: dark and light;

good and bad; male and female, etc. there are also negative energies in the fourth dimension that can frighten you. They may lull you into a feeling of false security, and then scare you or even harm you. This is why you shouldn't use a Ouija board, as they often bring in abusive negative spirits. It is much safer, if you contact a Master, your Guardian Angels, or Higher Self to talk to and learn from. Call in an Angel such as the Archangel Michael if you ever feel frightened or wary. His blue light and spiritual sword will often chase any negative entities away.

You can also manifest things in your life. For instance, you may want to go on a vacation to Australia. You may think about it a lot and imagine yourself there, enjoying the beach and wildlife. You may not have enough money or free time, to go on the vacation. A strange set of incidents may begin to occur. Your boss tells you to take your vacation earlier this year, as he will need you to work on a project later in the year. A coworker tells you that she is originally from Australia and is going there for a year. She invites you to come and stay with her family. You walk past a travel agency and see a special price on Australian airfares for the next few months. Do you see how you have effectively manifested your inexpensive accommodation, free time, and inexpensive airfares? You have done all this subconsciously. Now you need to learn how to consciously manifest what you want.

Here are some manifesting techniques:
1. Think of the object you want and ask that it come to you "for your highest good." (Being prepared to not have it manifest if it will do you harm instead of good, interfere with another person's freewill, or is not in the best interest of humanity).
2. Put an emotional feeling behind the image of what you want. Emotion helps to get it to you quicker. For instance - satisfaction, joy, happiness, contentment, and love.
3. Put a visual reminder of what you want in a prominent place,

such as an ad, picture, or drawing on your bedside table.

4. Imagine that you already have the object. Feel as if it is already part of your life.

5. Have faith that it is coming to you and release it to your angels and the Universe.

6. Detach from details that are absolute. For instance, if you want to manifest a red Toyota, don't knock back the offer of a green Toyota. You can always paint it red.

7. Be patient. The Universe will bring the object to you in Divine timing and it may not be by your deadline.

8. Be prepared to put some effort into attaining the object - save half the money, enter competitions, or ask and negotiate for it.

9. Be grateful and thank your angels and guides for their help and guidance.

End manifesting techniques

Early Star children born since the late 1960's have been born with their third eye chakras, pelvic chakras, and crown chakras open. This aids them with their psychic skills. They are easily able to develop telepathy, ESP, and spiritual contact. Unfortunately, most are not aware of their potential and many are confused, drug addicted, and disillusioned with life on Earth. However, everyone can develop his or her own abilities. These are natural, inherent psychic talents that we all have. But, as with most things in life, you have to learn about them, study, and practice them often, if you want to be good at them.

It should be noted that if you use your psychic gifts for bad things, you will be karmically responsible for all negative deeds that you do. You will either have to repay them in this life or in future lives. Not all pain in our lives is due to karmic pay back. It may be important to connect us to humanity or show us that we can have a life of pain and still be able to spiritually forgive, ascend, and have a great love and kindness in our hearts for all people in all walks of life.

Develop and use your psychic skills for something positive and constructive such as healing, teaching, assisting humanity, and guiding others.

By being tolerant, unconditionally loving, and caring of others, you can give people joy and direction in their lives. Try and detach from emotionally damaging situations. Observe others and see them as spirits acting out a play, in physical human bodies, unaware of the reasons behind their actions. Be kind and gentle towards them. Live your life with happiness and forgiveness and discover your heart and soul's purpose. Do not be overwhelmed and motivated by fear, as most people are. Take control of your life, in a firm but loving way. Live your beliefs and philosophy. Always trust in the Universe and know that you are loved and being guided, in the best possible way, towards your greatest potential, spiritual lessons, and life purpose.

One practical way of living as a spiritual being is by being very aware of each situation that arises in your life and not reacting emotionally towards it. When an argument arises, step back and look at everyone concerned. Think to yourself, "How would an angel or guide react?" With love, gentleness, and detachment. Not with anger, hate, or spite. Take gentle control or turn away, but don't retaliate. See the higher view and ask yourself, is this argument really important? Is there another way to deal with the issue? See your opponents as other lost spirits acting out of fear and forgive them and release the issue.

Try to see what makes you angry or upset, locate where this feeling comes from, and let it go from you forever. Release the problem to the Universe. Each time you do this, you will find it easier to do, so that soon it will become automatic.

Realize that everything happens for a reason in Divine timing. Think what you can learn from it, whether the experience seems good or bad. Treat everyone you know, whether it is the boss, principal, parent, child, spouse, or student with respect as they are all equal as souls. Honor yourself, as you are unique and valuable in life. You have gifts. Only you can develop your psychic abilities and raise your spiritual light, wherever you are.

Psychic Perception by Julia Jablonski

Julia Jablonski, ordained Spiritual minister, medium/clairvoyant, metaphysical author, and editor of Kajama talks about psychic perception.

There are subtle mental borderlines beyond which all conscious reason and understanding seem to fall away. It is in this gray area that we struggle to understand logically that which is beyond conventional reason. What is it that is accessed by a psychic? How do we know where to look for the answers? How do we even know there are answers?

At this time of rapid technological development, science has become the religion of the masses. Fortunately, new technology is also helping us to confirm much of what the mystics have known and taught for ages. There are ways of knowing that go beyond the left-brain, logical, mechanical approach that is emphasized in Western culture and cultivated in an educational structure that defines thought and "reality" in limiting ways.

For example, some of us have better physical vision than others. A child can spot an airplane far away in the sky that may not even "exist" for the child's great-grandmother. A dog can hear pitches above the human range of hearing. We can not hear it, but that does not mean it is less "real" than what we can hear. Modern technology has given us the ability to detect and measure energy that is usually beyond our physical awareness. Our physical eyes can detect color from red to violet, but we now know that infrared exists below the spectrum we're able to see, and ultra-violet exists above the frequency our eyes generally observe.

Psychics are not dealing with the "physical" universe as governed by known laws related to space and time, but are accessing non-physical information through non-physical senses. From a quantum physical perspective, there are no hard boundaries or limitations in the Universe, including those we generally perceive related to space and time. Our thoughts or conscious awareness can transcend the constructed "reality" of space/time in order to see into something at a "distance," or see into the future.

Many people ask how readers can read over the Internet, without a physical body present. Well, how can a psychic read when the person is not present? Unless a psychic is simply reading a person's body language, it should not make a difference. The energies and information accessed are not of the physical realm, and therefore not influenced by physical particulars. "Physical" here denotes that which is experienced by our physical senses. That which is seen, felt, heard, smelled, and tasted. There is truly nothing that is "solid" or "physical," as we tend to think of it. There is a range of vibrations that constitute what we call physical reality, and as we rise above this, we enter the non-physical, just as when we heat water, it goes from solid (ice) to liquid, to gas, and seems to "disappear." Psychics are able to continue to perceive the "gas" realm of energy that is not observable to others.

This extraordinary awareness is achieved by expanding or altering one's state of consciousness. What is perceived is then translated into words for communicating what has been observed or gleaned from the process. Just as some people are better able to see that airplane far off in the distance, so are others better able to transcend space and time consciously. While physical skills take a bit more work to influence, the development of psychic ability is similar to the development of any mental ability. Just as we can learn to paint or perform mathematics, so too can we develop the skills of the psychic arts. Of course, just as some are born natural artists or mathematicians, some are also born with the unique energy and genetic aptitude to be gifted psychics.

In addition to natural ability, it takes time, focus, and discipline for psychics to continue to develop and maintain their skills. Most devote time daily to meditation. Overall balance and clarity must be maintained in the entire energy system. All the chakras must be kept in harmony, so to work intensely with spirit means one must work comparably with higher dimensional energies. Blocks or clouded energy in one sphere will limit what one is able to achieve in the spiritual arena, and concurrently, the higher and clearer all aspects of the human energy system, the more deeply and powerfully one is able to work in any one area.

To achieve this balance, it's essential to nurture the physical body through exercise, healthy/natural food, and adequate sleep. Heart chakra energies must be kept clean and clear. This means acting with integrity, honesty, and compassion. It means working through the issues of the ego in order to truly come from the heart and be a clear channel of divine love and wisdom. The mind must also be honored and fed. It must be allowed to question, to analyze, and to learn and expand in knowledge and understanding. It must be kept open and fluid, receptive to change and new ideas. The body, heart, mind, and spirit are not separate, but like the organs of our body, specialize in different functions, and work together to make a whole.

Everyone has the raw capacity to access information psychically. Everyone is communicating with spirit and perceiving subtle energies and information at a less than conscious level all the time whether they realize it or not. The benefits of employing a psychic include having the opportunity to take advantage of that person's natural and developed ability, without having to spend years and a great deal of daily focus to achieve the same level of conscious awareness. All greatly successful people hire "specialists" to do what is beyond their own range of expertise.

While it is amazing and wonderful to be able to predict the future, it is a far greater gift to be able to use such a skill to empower people to create what they want in their lives. A psychic who works from the heart is truly a healer. Such a reader works not just to be accurate in predicting, but to empower and inspire the client to use the information provided to make decisions and take actions that will lead to where the client personally wants to go or is meant to go. The highest and most effective aim a reader or healer can have is to love another into well being and to hold an appreciative vision of that individual in perfect harmony and balance, having already achieved what he or she desires. By integrating the ability to foresee the future and channel guidance from Spirit along with an intention of empowering and inspiring others, a psychic can help those she or he serves to dramatically transform their lives for the better.

End Psychic Perception by Julia Jablonski

It is easy to believe in angels and guides when you hear, see, or receive messages from them. It is important to still believe in them even if you can't see or hear them. They are always with you and never stop trying to get messages of love and guidance to you.

So many people of Earth feel as though they have been left, that they are alone and there is no one to help them during troubled and difficult times. Angels and guides are always with you. Always within your touch, sight, and hearing offering gentle reminders of who you are and how to find your way. Follow your heart's and spiritual path and know you are never alone in the world.

Chapter 9
Teachers of Conscious Awareness

Generations to come will scarce believe that such a one as this walked the earth in flesh and blood...Albert Einstein

It is believed that Star children are coined this name because they have never incarnated here on earth before and may not have any karmic debts to pay. They are here on a special assignment with others to help aid us in a transition to a higher vibrational frequency and a new earth.

The Indigo, Crystal, and Rainbow children are here to confront us with realities on the level of our families and communities. They are forcing us, through their very presence, to wake up to what we are doing to ourselves and to the planet. They do this in the way of the spiritual warrior, by living their truth and making us aware of our truth.

For these beings of higher consciousness, incarnating on planet Earth at this time is an adventure. It is a "group project" in which thousands of these souls are arriving as teachers and healers for the human race.

They are here to wake us up and they do whatever they need to shock us into conscious awareness. But they are also here to have fun.

Star children generally don't see their mission in a heavy and "responsible" way, and for this reason they are quite often under-prepared and run into trouble with Earth systems and beliefs. It is the role of parents to assist them to understand the nature of life on Earth and to help them to create the fun and joy that they seek. We need to affirm to them that we are hearing them and are willing to help them with their "mission" of conscious evolution.

Special Note
The purpose of conscious evolution for the human species as a whole is to create a "New Earth." With the assistance of the Indigo, Crystal, and Rainbow children we, as a species, will rediscover our oneness, our common humanity.
End Special Note

This knowledge will be used to raise our consciousness and to begin to create a new Earth. This will be a place where every living being can thrive and be respected for what they are and where humans will learn to respect the similarities and the differences between them, and to live with loving tolerance of those differences. In fact, to celebrate the incredible diversity that characterizes our "oneness" and makes life an "adventure" in consciousness. Peace must also be made within us in order to make peace in the world.

The children that are here are teachers of conscious awareness. These children seem somehow smarter, brighter, and wiser. They are attracted to and easily master difficult and complex technologies. They are passionate, focused, and honest about their feelings.

The first teachers of conscious awareness to arrive were the Indigo children. They are spiritual warriors whose function is to clear the old systems so that something new can be created. They are the systems busters who will liberate us from our old ways of thinking.

They do this by incarnating into our families and communities. They bring with them their gifts of advanced spiritual development, a high level of consciousness, and wisdom. They are spiritually aware and awake and refuse to allow themselves to be constrained or enslaved by impersonal systems.

They show us that gentle, wise, and high-level beings cannot flourish and thrive in the systems we have created. The high level of adolescent and teenage dysfunction among Indigo children in our society is a signal that our society is dysfunctional and needs to change to accommodate beings of higher ability.

The Indigo children are the trailblazers, the ones who shock us into awareness and instigate change. An even more powerful group, the Crystal children, follows them. These children are warriors of the heart. They are here to teach us the ways of love and peace.

Crystal children are considered to be fully developed masters who carry the Christ consciousness seed within them. This term denotes a being that is aware of his or her connection with a Divine source and chooses to live in harmony with this knowing.

Because they function at such a high level of consciousness, these children are extremely sensitive both to their environment and to the feelings and emotions of others. They have come to teach us about tolerance, respect for others, and how to care for our home.

The Rainbow children are the third generation of special children that have come to help humanity evolve. The purpose of the Rainbow children is to complete the final stages of the foundation that the Indigo and Crystal children have made.

Karma is very important when teaching conscious awareness. Every thought that you have, every word that you speak either adds to or takes away from the light of humanity. Everything that you think and say about yourself, whether it is silently to yourself or aloud to others, either adds to or takes away from the light of humanity. Everything that you think and say to and about others, whether it is silently to yourself or aloud to others, either adds to or takes away from the light of humanity. There are no insignificant thoughts or words, each one has an energy and an effect.

When your thoughts and words come from a space of unconditional love, which means that they are without judgment, they spread light and increase the light and vibrational frequency on the planet. But when they come from fear or anger, they take away from the light. Yes, your thoughts and words do make a difference and each one is important. Even the smallest judgment thought that you have has an effect. Each person is as important as another is in spreading the light to others.

Just as you are discovering your power to create miracles and manifest your reality, you must also realize that this power extends to all parts of being, including and especially your thoughts and words. You do not have insignificant thoughts, so guard your thoughts and words. We must all release anger, fear, and judgement from our lives. These feelings block our energy and keep us at a lower vibrational frequency, on the old energy grid, and keep us from ascending.

Learning to let go of old, bad energy patterns and adapting to change is also important for conscious awareness. Reaction to change is often tinged with suspicion and caution, or resistance. Adapting to change involves give and take. You have to let go of something to gain something. Holding on to old stuff or old energy can block your aura and slow down your progression.

On a spiritual level, bad emotions and issues block energy. Often, we have old issues tying up emotional fields and energy and our bodies don't want to take on one more issue. We are overloaded with stuff, so to speak.

As a result, the subconscious finds every excuse as to why we should not deal with whatever it is we should deal with. Our subconscious is protecting us from having to deal with emotional issues and fears surrounding these old negative energy patterns.

Realizing core issues, the stuff we are hanging on to that we don't need to hang on to, will help our energy patterns. It is important in understanding conscious awareness that we must forgive. Forgiveness allows the release of all old pain and then the current issues suddenly don't seem so overwhelming.

Stuffing down real emotions out of love for another can cause us to feel resentment toward both the individuals causing the pain and ourselves for getting into the situation to begin with. We allow old emotions to be released, making room for new and better energy, when we release our expectations of perfection both toward ourselves and others.

If we think of the emotional body, or auric field, like a hard drive, there is only so much memory it can hold on to before it starts to freeze up when running big programs. Releasing these old programs and pains from the past makes room for better newer programs to be installed.

Great beauty and opportunity are within everyone with conscious awareness, even deep beneath old scars and betrayals. Forgiveness is the foundation of all spiritual work and growth because it is through awareness that one can truly really know your own life's journey and perspective.

Forgiveness is not a process of giving out something to another person who may not deserve anything, but is instead a process of turning our energy inward and using the power of love to really look at our relationships with others and ourselves.

When anchored in forgiveness, we are all within the spiritual realm of conscious awareness rather than in the realm of emotions or the mind.

It is natural to release old energy because holding on to it hinders the flow of love into your own life and blocks your own spiritual balance and peace. Love is the energy that gives and maintains life. Forgiving others, even those who don't seem to deserve it, can bring life-giving energy into your body.

Love also binds us to all other humans. The issues that seem to defy forgiveness are always about love. Love that we never received, love offered but rejected or betrayed, and love used as manipulation or control. These are all old issues tied to love and forgiveness.

By tying your spiritual energy reserves up into old hurts, you are limiting the amount of vibrational energy of love available in the present moment. Each morning or evening can be spent reviewing any old emotions or hurts from the day that you are carrying around and praying through them, letting them go from your spiritual light.

We all have stuff in our auras and in our hearts that create challenges and blockages in our lives, holding us back from conscious awareness. We are all in the process of learning how to clear these issues, entities, thought forms, fears, and old wounds from our bodies so that we can all ascend and become the enlightened beings that we are meant to be.

Star children are teaching us that conscious awareness can also be obtained through faith. Great teachers of the world, such as Buddha, derived their strength and inspiration not from muscle or intellect, but from faith.

Buddha spoke a great language that went straight to people's hearts. Star children are no different. They speak and connect to us through their heart chakras and ask us to have faith.

Hollywood child star Shirley Temple Black once narrated an incident about her husband Charles and his mother. When Charles was a boy he asked his Mom what was the happiest moment in her life. His mother replied, "This moment, right now." The boy further asked, "But what about all the other happy moments in your life, say, when you were married?" His mother replied, "My happiest moment then, was then. My happiest moment now is now. You can live your life only in the moment you are in and this requires unflinching faith."

The mission of lightworkers is to teach us to be a light to ourselves and to others. Star children are here to build and spread the light for all of humanity. This is why they are here at this critical time in humanity's evolution.

You can be a light and spread your own light by focusing your intention on what you want in your life. Those who focus on what others have are seeing their lives from a point of lack. By focusing your energy on what you want, you bring the light into your life and then spread the light to others. Each of you is important to the task that you have come to do. The result of your energy is continuously manifested all around you. Take this power that has been taught to us by Star children and use it wisely, for you have come to spread the light to the world. Use it well and create heaven on earth, for yourselves and for all of humanity through conscious awareness.

Chapter 10
Star Parents
(Parenting Star Children)

I think, at a child's birth, if a mother could ask a fairy godmother to endow it with the most useful gift, that gift should be curiosity...Eleanor Roosevelt

Star children want to change the world for the better in many ways. They want to wake us up to the fact that we have angels and guides who are trying to help us and guide us. They want to work for a more peaceful and we are "one" attitude of the world. They may be working hard to spread compassion to those who have less and to help these people. They may also be helping our environment or animals in many ways.

Whatever their mission, they need help from their parents. Parents of Star children need to look at their kids and ask themselves, "How can I help my child achieve their purpose in life?" Parents may not be able to help their children's life be easier or better but they can help their children set their goals and help them to help others in need.

Star children may choose a path in life that parents would not choose for their children. As parents of Star children, you must remember that they have a definite path to follow and it may not be what you want it to be. In the end, they will do what they want to do because that is what they came here to do.

We also can not put our children in a box. They are here to make a new path that will be better for humanity and the world as we know it. If we can validate our children and accept them as the new "normal," we can allow them to develop their gifts naturally in a timely manner with guidance and encouragement.

Advice from Eri Morningstar

Eri Morningstar mentions a few things for parents of Star children to consider:

Don't talk down to psychic kids or their empathetic gifts as they have complex emotional bodies and electrical systems. Remember they are very ancient souls in little bodies, and their minds work in a way that is different than adults, but definitely not in the way children's minds have worked in the past. They think on several levels at once and are aware of the mass consciousness grid reality, other dimensional realities, and parallel worlds.

A three-year-old psychic child may understand "A Midsummer Night's Dream" from Shakespeare or the legends of King Arthur just as easily as "Barney," and will probably prefer the former.

They can tap into the energy grids and come up with that understanding instantly. The vastness of their being is sometimes a bit overwhelming for the youngest ones, their vibrations are so high and they are so open, empathic, and sensitive that they "pick up" on emotions around them and get to overload points every now and then. Even though their minds and emotional/electrical systems are very advanced compared to ours, their emotional bodies are still developed at the level of their physical age. So your two-year-old peaceful, loving and psychic toddler will at some point have her two-year-old emotional body overloaded and then irritability and tantrums may set in.

I have found with my two-year-old daughter that what she needs most at a time of overload is peace and quiet, so she can settle down her electrical system and ground again. Sometimes Reiki and singing quietly while rocking in the rocking chair helps, or lying down in a quiet dimmed room for 10 minutes. I can sense right away when she is centered again. I have noticed that this gets worse during times of intense solar flare activity and magnetic storms. Some of the little ones are very connected to the Earth Christ Grid, Crystallines grids, and/or axiotonal and ley line grids.

Watch the weather sites for information on solar and magnetic activity and then help guide your psychic toddlers through those times gracefully. It helps to explain to them what is happening as well. Show them photos of the sun and the earth, and if you can find photos of the solar activity online, then show them that as well. Explain how the magnetics affect their emotional systems and let them know they can ask their higher self and angels for help when the energy around them gets wild.

They will get it, and will be able to make adjustments themselves to keep there little bodies balanced, which will make your job easier.

End Advice from Eri Morningstar

Parenting a Star child isn't easy. It is a time for change and new energy on this planet and parent-child relationships are more important now than ever. These children will mirror everything that is in a parent's heart and mind. Changing old parenting paradigms will help these special children grow into healthy well-adjusted adults.

Confronting Old Rules – A Star Parent Story

My three-year-old is one of the most independent and freedom-loving toddlers I have ever seen. As soon as he could walk, he ran, and he ran and ran and ran - right out of the yard and down the dirt road in front of our farm.

The normal boundaries that most babies feel or sense didn't apply to him. As long as the wind was blowing in his long hair, he would run with a huge smile on his face, usually buck-naked to boot. Whenever he was in the yard playing, we could not look away even for a moment.

Most toddlers at the barely-walking age are content with toddling around the yard exploring little things here and there, always keeping one eye on Mommy or Daddy as they check out new things little by little. But my toddler just ran out into the world. He couldn't wait to see everything. We knew the normal boundaries were not going to apply in his life. We could tell him to stay in the yard until our faces were blue, but it would do no good. It is not a part of who he is or why he is here.

So we let him run, and would just run along after him when he got too far. As a little sister and brother were born, I could not run as far or as fast after him and then we had to come up with new ways of giving him his freedom, while still keeping him safe. Eventually, we had to fence in our farm, where we sit on a five-acre plot. The new boundary we compromised was that he can run as much as he wants with little overbearing supervision within the yard, unless we go with him to explore. Our toddler was happy with this as he got more unsupervised freedom for his creative imagination and play, and no standing rules of behavior. We were happy knowing he would not be out in the road anymore.

Old rules cannot be imposed on psychic kids, even the littlest ones. Get used to compromising and finding ways to meet your kid's needs while still keeping them safe. They will push the envelope always. After all, that is why they are here. So give them a great big envelope to push. If you set rules and boundaries like you had as a child or like a normal kid would have, their frustrations will build.

End Confronting Old Rules – A Star Parent Story

Star children have come to the planet with their own mission. As an Indigo, they are here to challenge existing forms and beliefs. As a Crystal, they are here to teach empowerment and love and as a Rainbow, they are here to build on what the Indigo and Crystal children have begun. You, as the parents, are the partners in this mission of teaching and healing. You can help your child to fulfill his or her mission by understanding what is required of you.

As the parent of an Indigo, you can expect to be challenged at every turn. Having the skills to handle these challenges will create an easier relationship between you and your Indigo. As the parent of a Crystal, you will have to deal with a very strong will and frequent power struggles. As the parent of a Rainbow, you will have to deal with hyperactivity and a child with high energy. Again, having the parenting skills to cope with these issues will facilitate the growth and unfolding of your child.

Parenting Indigo Children
Wendy H. Chapman, Director of Metagifted Education Resource Organization gives some advice on parenting Indigo children:

Even Indigos have to be disciplined. If they're not, they will walk all over you. Please don't misunderstand me - I don't mean punished, I mean they need to learn what is acceptable behavior and what is not and learn not to do the unacceptable things. Be fair, but set appropriate limits. Set reasonable consequences for not having them followed. For instance, a five-minute time out instead of "you'll be sorry," which is too vague, or "I'm going to thrash you," which you hopefully don't mean. Follow through. If possible, allow the children to help you set the limits. For instance, have them tell you where it isn't safe to play. You can guide this discussion to what you need and have them help determine the consequences, which will probably be harsher than yours would be. They might say that they shouldn't be allowed to play with their favorite toy all the next day whereas you might have said for a half-hour. In this way, they are helping to set the rules and will hopefully help to follow them, too.

Give reasons for why your child is not allowed to do something, like run around wild or yell at the top of his voice; "Please stop yelling, it's hurting Mommy and kitty's ears." Indigos need to know where you're coming from even if they don't like it. It's important that they hear it.

Give choices "A or B - not C." If he doesn't choose, he doesn't get either. Tell him the truth as much as the age will allow. Don't ever lie to a Star child. They know. Tell him he's loved and hug him a lot.

If you and your spouse argue, make sure the kids know it's not their fault. Kids usually think they are the cause of arguing in the home even when it has nothing to do with them. To them, the world does revolve around them, so they have to be told that you still love them. Give them extra love and attention after this because the extra stress will be very difficult for them. Often, Indigos are empathetic, which will make it even more difficult for them to be in stressful situations. Play music to help change the mood and energy in a place. You can also use incense, make cookies, or go for a walk.

Indigos are very explorative and have tons of energy. It helps if you channel this into something fun, productive, or at least not dangerous.

If your children are old enough, you can send them on a scavenger hunt to find nature things such as a rock with a stripe on it, two leaves almost alike, 6 acorns, a bug, a wildflower, running water, 6 leaves all of different colors, etc. Children enjoy nature and will like this sort of entertainment. You can go with them, too. You'll be surprised what else you find out in the yard.

Make cleaning up (their toys and games) their responsibility. You can help, but they should do most of it. You can also make it into a game by singing or playing a song and seeing if they can finish it all by the time the song ends and maybe get a little reward if they do. Mostly it will help for them to know why they need to clean up, how to do it, and that the making it into a game isn't to make them do it, since it has to be done, but just to help make it fun once in awhile.

Parenting a Star child is a special privilege in this time of energy change. As a parent, you are contributing to establishing new patterns for parenting on the planet. You are partnering with your child in raising the resonance of the parent–child relationship to its highest possible level at this time.

End Wendy H. Chapman gives some advice on parenting Indigo children

In the past, the old parenting paradigm was based largely on power and fear. The parent saw the child as a responsibility that had to be undertaken, and the parental duty was to ensure that the child was provided for materially, educated, and formed into an adult just like all the other adults. The child was brought up to fear punishment and to see parents, teachers, and other adults as power figures. The child was taught to accept the norms of society by these power figures, even if these went against his or her natural inclinations and the parents and caregivers saw their role as one of control over the child. They therefore felt entitled to punish the child, even with violence, if that control, usually exerted in the form of rules and prohibitions, was challenged or ignored. The point of the rules and regulations was to ensure that the child would "fit in" or conform to society. Old style parents often say things like, "You will do it because I said so, and because I'm your mother/father."

The old style parent is an authoritarian and demands compliance and respect on the basis of that authority vested in the parent/child relationship. In this belief system, the parents seem to own the child and have the right to demand compliance. The parents believe themselves to know more and to be wiser, and therefore have the right to demand certain behavior patterns and life choices from their child.

The old parenting paradigm just will not work for Star children. They are here to challenge this paradigm and to replace it with something better. The way you were brought up will not work for them and you cannot repeat these old parenting patterns.

The new parenting paradigm is based on love and is derived from the heart center. In this new paradigm, every child is seen as a gift and a privilege. Parenting is viewed as a heart experience, in which the adult is given the mission of nurturing and assisting a newly arrived soul to the planet. This mission is a partnership in which the parent and the child share the adventure of creating the conscious experience of growth and learning.

In this new heart-based parenting paradigm, the child is seen as a highly evolved and developed soul. These Star children have their own wisdom to contribute to humanity, and the parent's role is to help the Star child bring their message and wisdom to the world.

Qualities such as love, tolerance, respect, and unconditional acceptance need to be part of basic parenting in the new parenting paradigm. Also, the new parent needs to learn and understand the skills of negotiation, communication, and discipline. You must love and respect yourself in order to love and respect your child. Many people were brought up with messages of not being good enough. This caused low self-esteem and difficulties with self-love and self-acceptance. Parents with there own unresolved self-acceptance issues need to be careful that these issues are not projected onto their children. Star children will easily pick up on this energy and may act out in a naughty, unmanageable, or out of control manner as a result.

Also, a parent's unresolved anger and hostility are often reflected back to that parent in the Star child's behavior. Often an angry and temperamental child will play out the repressed feelings of a parent.

It is difficult to raise a Star child unless you have worked through your own issues and are able to love yourself, empower yourself, and express your full potential.

Unconditional love and acceptance are some of the most difficult things for a parent. Star children have their own defined being and their own sense of who and what they are. Sometimes, this sense of who they are can be in direct opposition to the parent's desires and needs. When this happens, it takes a very special parent to be able to say, "I accept you for what you are," and "You do not need to be like me."

The new parent allows their children to unfold and be what they are, even encouraging aspects of the child's being that may be foreign to their own way of thinking or being if that is where the child's gifts lie.

The new parent also accepts that as their Star child grows into adolescence and adulthood, they may not choose to follow the safe and responsible career paths that many parents wish. The Indigo child may wish to be creative, or travel the world and see life, rather then go to college and follow a set life path.

New parents will need to understand that Star children see life as an ongoing creation, where they are free to remake themselves whenever they feel as they follow their passions.

It is important not to be violent with your Star child, ever. This just teaches the child that violence is a tool for getting what you want. The concept of discipline is poorly understood in our society. It is equated with rules, regulations, and punishment.

Your role as a Star parent is to teach your child, through example and through words, what is required of them to become empowered and loving adults. You are the teacher and they are the students. Sometimes, they are the teachers and you, as parents, are the students.

Since the Universe does not make mistakes, we can look at the situation as the way things are evolving during ascension, and can stop judging and criticizing ourselves as parents as there is no such thing as accidents.

The lessons during the shift in consciousness are to learn to imagine love for ourselves and for the world. The only thing that we need in our lives is love, for out of love everything else is manifested. If we learn to love everyone and everything, we can and will change the path of humanity. Imagine love in your life, both internally and externally. Detach from every judgment about everyone and everything and just imagine the energy of love filling every part of your life. Imagine love and the loving relationships you desire will manifest in your life.

This is as a reminder to all Star parents of special children who have psychic gifts or have sensitive energy. Don't load them up with your expectations of what they should be or do. They are beautiful souls who have potential to bloom into something wonderful.

Star children may show gifts in one area, and not another. They may seem to excel at one thing, but fail at something else. Pushing doesn't help these sensitive children. Encouragement does.

In order for Star children to grow into their purpose, they need to know they are loved exactly as they are and not for what they might become.

Help your children to understand things that are difficult for them. Let them explore areas to find out where their interest's best lie and discover their life's purpose.

Star children and all other gifted or special kids are still children. They need boundaries and rules just like all children. They need to be held accountable for what they agree to do, and be appreciated for what they do accomplish no matter how big or small these accomplishments are. If you can provide an atmosphere of loving acceptance for their gifts or special ways without having to name them as something exceptional or different, it will help them to sprout into their very best selves.

Do your part as a loving and guiding parent for your special child. In time, Star children will find their life's purpose, and you will have helped as a Star parent because you gave your child a bright light on their path of life.

Chapter 11
The Nine Dimensions of Consciousness

The more original a discovery, the more obvious it seems afterwards...Arthur Koestler

Dimensions are the fundamental building blocks of reality. We live in a conscious universe because the universe was created entirely from original consciousness. Every aspect of the universe, from stars to humans and even sunlight, are all composed of original consciousness.

Dimensions include the three dimensions of space (length, breadth, and height), time, thought, feeling, and the three fundamental energies which make up physical and non-physical matter (etheric, magnetic, and electric).

Every physical object has three size dimensions (length, breadth and height) and exists at a specific location in space at a certain point in time. Matter, on the other hand, is constructed of varying amounts of electro-magnetic force. This means that both electrical energy and magnetic energy are fundamental building blocks within the physical world.

Human consciousness consists of the fundamental building blocks of thought and feeling. These are also dimensions of reality. Consciousness goes far beyond the realm of human thought.

103

Dimensions are measurable items, the variables of the universe. For example, space consists of three dimensions (length, breadth, and height) and time is referred to as the fourth dimension.

Time is not just linear flow, as in the river of time. It is the dimension that brings physical motion into existence. The glass arrived upon the tabletop at some point in time, and it will leave the tabletop at another point in time. When it leaves it will be exhibiting motion through space.

Until recently, all people born on Earth were born as third dimensional beings. This means that they were born on the material plane or realm, and their consciousness was locked into the third dimension. This dimension functions on the first three chakras; the material, the emotional, and the mental.

The third dimensional soul is aware of himself or herself as a separate and unique individual. There is no real sense of the unity or oneness of consciousness that is a factor of higher dimensional consciousness. Because of this sense of separation, people have built a society that has very little awareness of the interconnectedness of others. Due to this lack of awareness, people have created a planet of sorrow and suffering, where individuals see no need to be responsible for their thoughts, feelings, and actions.

There are many dimensions of consciousness. Some people may have heard of nine or twelve dimensions. Barbara hand Clow says there are actually over twenty dimensions. However, Earth is a realm that holds nine dimensions of consciousness that all humans can access.

The first dimension of consciousness is the realm of the iron core crystal in the center of the earth. This dimension grounds us and provides protection. This is the primary and most fundamental feature of human consciousness. An example would be up and down, on and off, change and no change, and yin and yang. The first dimension corresponds with the color red, which is the first color in the light spectrum. Red is the color of "one".

The second dimension is the realm of life between the earth's core and the surface of the Earth. This consists of crystalline, metallic, chemical essences, and the denser world of minerals and microbes. This dimension regulates all of our autonomic body processes. Our health is contingent with our connection to this dimension. The second dimension expands on the first with the invention of relationships and grouping, such as black and white or rich and poor. In this dimension, there are areas of dark, light, and shades of gray. In the visible spectrum, orange is the second hue, conveying an energetic cooling off from the intensity of red.

The third dimension is the material realm in which we live in linear space and time. It is associated with the earth's surface and our physicality. It deals with linear space and time and human consciousness.

The third dimension is what we live in. It includes all life on Earth and their relationships with each other. The third dimension relates to three dimensional space or volume. The third dimension is a progression from the flat "two" universe, which allows us to introduce "depth" for the creation of the infinity of forms, textures, molecules, and characteristics. These make up the experiences we have in our world. The color that corresponds to the third dimension is yellow.

The Indigo children arrived with the key to multi-dimensionality. They were born into third dimensional bodies, but their consciousness was effectively in the fourth dimension and capable of moving into the fifth. When the first big wave of Indigo consciousness arrived on the planet in the early 1970s, the way was opened for all humans and the planet itself, to shift into the fourth dimension.

The fourth dimension deals with "time." The universe is a cycle on top of a cycle on top of a cycle. Time is nothing more than a circle that is repeating. You can stop on a point in time, go forward on a point in time, and go backward on a point in time, since it is nothing more than a point on a circle. It is infinite, with no beginning and no end. Green is the color that corresponds to the fourth dimension.

The fourth dimension is the material realm of dark and light forces that forms our mind-body polarities, especially from our emotions. This dimension deals with the collective realm of thoughts and feelings emanating from all living things. It bridges the seen and unseen worlds. The fourth dimension represents time, not in the sense of calendars or clocks, but in the sense of the field or stage upon which all three-dimensional interactions are played out.

At the fourth dimensional level of consciousness, humans become aware of the Universal Law of One, otherwise known as universal consciousness. This law states that we are all one and we are all connected. Whatever affects one of us, affects all of us. Star children carry this awareness in their consciousness making them warriors for many causes that will heal the earth and stop people from destroying and polluting their environment and harming each other.

The law of one also fosters the understanding in Star children that we are all equal and that no one person is greater than any other. This group consciousness and group awareness is the path to the future for people. Learning to function co-operatively and for the good of all is important in creating the new earth that we desire.

The fifth dimension is the electromagnetic field of energy that centers in the heart. It deals with love and creativity in dimensions of light. The fifth dimension identifies organic life as having properties that are separate and progressed from the inorganic universe. While a rock can be here or there, large or small, heavy or light, older or newer, only a living creature can be healthy, sick, hungry, content, in pain or in comfort.

The fifth dimension can measure pain and pleasure. In our lives, we understand the fifth dimension as the sensation of touch. Five deals with chaotic inclination (chaos theory), human manifestation of the fire element called spirit, and the higher resonance of the number "one." It also deals with the realm of love.

When a Star child's awareness opens into the fifth dimension, the child becomes aware of himself or herself as a creator. Fifth dimensional awareness loves to create. All the religious belief systems and the economic systems on Earth today are fifth dimensional creations that we hold in place by our continued support of these thought forms. They form a fifth dimensional grid around the Earth.

When the Star child's awareness opens to this level, there is often a rejection of all belief systems and a consciousness and freedom to create new and alternative ways of thinking and being. The Star child takes on the planetary mission of creating and bringing in new ways of thinking and being for the Earth. The next step in consciousness is to move beyond duality and into a realm where all is seen as part of the greater good and for the good of the greater whole. The color that corresponds to the fifth dimension is sky blue.

The sixth dimension is the realm where the heart's field manifests as sacred geometry, attributing a religious or cultural value to mathematical relationships. It deals with morphic fields and templates for the third dimension. The sixth dimension picks up where the fifth leaves off, just as the sixth color indigo is a deepening of sky blue. The sixth dimension is the sense of sight. Sight is the way organisms touch each other without actually touching each other.

The sixth dimension can be measured in joy and sadness. A human can transmit an amazing array of feelings and emotions by simply being looked at, or through mental telepathy. Six deals with love, hate, trust, pride, friendship, color, personality, memories, and communication with our natural world. Six deals with the "third eye," or the pineal gland, and the experience of healing. The color that corresponds with the sixth dimension is deep blue.

This advanced state is known as sixth-dimensional consciousness. It is the realm of the Christen Child or Magical Child. All Crystal children are born into this level of awareness. They have immediate access to the magical and spiritual aspects of who they are and are able to blend imagination and creation in fantastic and joyous ways. If they were left to their own devices, they would immediately manifest a magical planet. This can be difficult for them because they have to deal with a largely third dimensional consciousness and they may struggle with the patterns and behaviors they encounter.

The mature Crystal consciousness can move into the seventh dimensional level, where awareness opens onto the nature of the spiritual mission of the soul. At this level, a Star child is on a planetary mission to carry higher dimensional consciousness to others. The souls at this level are involved with teaching and healing on a grand scale. They may also carry the higher vibrational energy in their auric fields so that others may access the higher vibrations in their own upward ascension path.

The seventh dimension is the realm where the galactic highways of light and the sacred geometrical fields merge. This galactic information highway of light creates cosmic sounds that are the templates for the sixth dimension. It is the Galaxy's communication system.

If six is the natural world, seven extends to the supernatural. It includes extra sensory perception, prophecy, and precognition. Seven deals with fact and faction. The color that corresponds to the seventh dimension is violet.

The Star child now carries the potential to open fully to the ninth level or Full Christ Consciousness. This incorporates the eighth level, or Archetypal level, where the soul has full control over the story of their life on earth, and the ninth level, where the soul assumes full responsibility for stewardship of the planet.

The eighth dimension is the realm where the light (divine intelligence) gathers into galactic councils for guidance. It is the cosmic ordering for the galactic federation, the organization directed by the Orion star system that runs the eighth dimension. The color that corresponds to the eighth dimension is red but an octave higher on the vibrational frequency than the dimension.

The ninth dimension is the center of the Milky Way galaxy where the council of light exists. It is the origination of time. The ninth dimension is where we live. It is the place where all the colors of the spectrum can be seen as separate and united.

These nine dimensions are accessible by all people on our planet. These dimensions help us expand our universal consciousness. Star children of today want to be multidimensional. They demonstrate this by what they wear, the way they talk, and how they stand up to injustice and the wrongs of our archaic systems. We should all be asking ourselves: who are we, why are we here, and what is our role on this planet? Accessing dimensional consciousness will help answer these questions.

Chapter 12
A Global Crisis: Help is On the Way

If we have no peace, it is because we have forgotten that we belong to each other…Mother Teresa

Mahatma Gandhi once said that an "eye for an eye" would leave everybody blind. It is no secret that our planet has reached a global crisis as we are living among systems that no longer serve the good of humanity.

If we take a close look at the world around us, we can see that the world is becoming more impoverished. The rich are getting richer and the poor are getting poorer and taken advantage of. It is wonderful to have the things we need in life, but never forget that we all share a common home, our planet.

We continue to fill our landfills and fail to recycle, trashing our planet in the name of development. This is one reason the Star children have been sent here. They are the spiritual warriors who have come here to help shift our consciousness. These special children will help shift our world to a place where peace and love will change the planet.

It is more important now than ever to help nurture these special children. Without them, we are all going to hell in a handbasket, so to speak.

In order to understand why these children have come to Earth, we need to understand why their special gifts are needed at this time. Our planet has reached a crisis of epoch proportions. We, as her children, have reached a point of stagnation in our growth. We have hemmed ourselves in with systems that have become impersonal and no longer function for the greater good of humanity.

More and more of the worlds people are becoming impoverished in both material and spiritual terms, as a small minority accumulate more power and wealth for themselves. We continue to trash our planet in the name of development and to kill each other in senseless wars, often fought in the name of religion and freedom.

It is into this situation that the Indigo, Crystal, and Rainbow children have been sent. By shifting our consciousness, they are here to make us aware of what we are doing to ourselves and how we need to change our community life in order to create more nourishing, peaceful, and loving situations that will foster our continued growth as humans.

Star children's minds think differently. They process emotions differently, their energies are different, and they have incredible visions, promise, and hope. They also have amazing psychic and healing abilities. These children are stronger and better than we are. They can heal without medicine, they can ferret out lies and deceptions with their psychic abilities, and yes, they can help us save humanity. God knows we need to be saved by someone.

The energy of Star children is gaining interest for our attention. It is important to listen and be aware of the spiritual lessons they have to give us. Children are our greatest teachers. This is important to remember as these wise souls are here on a voluntary group mission for us.

The Star children have come to the planet to be your children. But they have come with a specific purpose – to help the planet with its evolution by raising our energy and consciousness. So while you may enjoy them and experience them as part of your family and your community, remember that they have a higher spiritual purpose.

As individuals, the Indigo, Crystal, and Rainbow children have many advanced gifts and talents. Often they are highly intelligent, creative, and psychic. They can see and communicate with guides and angels. As a group, their energy and their messages are important. As groups they are working on the planet to slowly bring in and ground a new kind of energy.

The message of the Star children is a message of the heart. As a group, they are working to help humanity open its collective heart chakra and embrace higher energy and higher consciousness. They are also creating a new society based on love and empowerment. It is a society that exists beyond duality, in the realm of oneness.

Our troubled world is in a state of crisis. The systems that have been set up by humans to create a stable society have become stagnant and repressive. Systems such as economics, health, law, and education are no longer serving communities and the people that they were originally designed to serve. These systems have become self-serving and are now destructive and harmful. These systems are fueled by greed and money. The government is run by big companies and their lobbyists, and this no longer serves the good of humanity.

Humanity, in general, has lost the spiritual dimension of life and is focused on the lower chakra areas of money, sex, and power. Consumption has become the goal of life in the developed world. Those beliefs and concepts are spreading around the planet producing a society based on greed and materialism and not one of unity and oneness.

The Star children have been brought in to align us with higher consciousness. They are psychic, spiritual, connected to the angelic realm, and happy to be working towards creating peace on earth.

As the first Star children were born all around the planet, their mission was to begin the process of questioning and challenging archaic systems. Many of these early Indigos served as leaders and facilitators for the shift of consciousness to the new energy grid.

These pioneering Indigos paved the way for the first big wave of Indigos. These Indigos began to raise the energy on the planet. As each new Indigo, Crystal, or Rainbow child is born, the level of consciousness on the planet is raised. When large numbers of them incarnate together, the energy is raised at an accelerated pace.

As early Crystal children began to arrive, the planet's new energy grid system was becoming more advanced. These children are grounded into the new energy grid system at a higher vibrational frequency. In time, all children will be born into the new energy grid and the old grid will fall away.

Finally, the Rainbow children will spread the works that have been built by Indigos and Crystals and make us aware of dimensional consciousness and the sense of oneness.

Through our Star children, we are learning the skills of intention, focus, and manifestation and we are also learning that the true meaning of happiness is not individual greed, but a collective need for sharing and an appreciation of oneness.

If there is one thing we have always had and always will have, it is hope. Hope is the most incredible word. This word not only means to wish for something, but to wait with expectation for its fulfillment. It is an emotional belief in a positive outcome related to events and circumstances within one's personal life. It is a belief that there will be a positive outcome even when there is evidence to the contrary.

As lightworkers, it is important to hold the light not only on us, but also on those who will not, or don't know how to, change their energy. We all made an agreement before we were born as to what our purpose is and how we were going to live out our lives to achieve that purpose and help humanity. We don't know what these agreements are for others or what role they chose to play in the Divine Plan of things. So be careful not to judge others and be kind to all, even people who are not kind to you and you will be truly happy.

About the Author

Nikki Pattillo graduated from Stephen F. Austin State University in Texas and began her career as a clinical and molecular biologist. She is the author of Children of the Stars: Advice for Parents and Star Children and also writes numerous newspaper articles to help raise awareness in consciousness on both environmental and spiritual issues.

As a child, Nikki was psychic conversing regularly with her angels and guides. This natural gift was not understood by her family or friends and consequently she shut down her abilities out of fear. It was these same angels and guides that came to her later in life and said that it was time for her to allow her gifts to grow stronger and open a path for others, especially children, to follow in peace and harmony and without fear of their gifts.

Children of the Stars: Advice for Parents and Star Children was written as a guide to help parents understand their Star children and to help each parent spiritually understand what is happening with these gifted children who are here to help us. It was written to help children understand and not be fearful of seeing and hearing things that others cannot see or hear.

Nikki says, "The most wonderful aspect of Star children is their willingness to take on the world and learn to make their own way through it. Star children will get to the point where they are able to mold society into something that reflects their energies and values. The truth that they hold and defend so well will reflect their integrity and spirituality and change the world as we know it."

Together with her husband Charlie and daughter Maddy, Nikki and her family live on a small island in the Gulf of Mexico where they can connect with dolphin energies and the elementals of nature. Nikki works with many charities and is president of the recycling committee of her local community. She also writes a column in the newspaper on various environmental and spiritual issues.

To contact the author, visit: www.starchildren.info

Other Books Published
by
Ozark Mountain Publishing, Inc.

Conversations with Nostradamus, Volume I, II, III..........by Dolores Cannon
Jesus and the Essenes..by Dolores Cannon
They Walked with Jesus...by Dolores Cannon
Between Death and Life... by Dolores Cannon
A Soul Remembers Hiroshima...by Dolores Cannon
Keepers of the Garden..by Dolores Cannon
The Legend of Starcrash..by Dolores Cannon
The Custodians...by Dolores Cannon
The Convoluted Universe - Book One, Two, Three.........by Dolores Cannon
I Have Lived Before..by Sture Lönnerstrand
The Forgotten Woman..by Arun & Sunanda Gandhi
Luck Doesn't Happen by Chance.............................by Claire Doyle Beland
Mankind - Child of the Stars........................by Max H. Flindt & Otto Binder
The Gnostic Papers...by John V. Panella
Past Life Memories As A Confederate Soldier...................by James H. Kent
Holiday in Heaven..by Aron Abrahamsen
Is Jehovah An E.T.?...by Dorothy Leon
The Ultimate Dictionary of Dream Language....................by Briceida Ryan
The Essenes - Children of the Light.........by Stuart Wilson & Joanna Prentis
Rebirth of the Oracle...........................by Justine Alessi & M. E. McMillan
Reincarnation: The View from Eternityby O.T. Bonnett, M.D. & Greg Satre
The Divinity Factor...by Donald L. Hicks
What I Learned After Medical School ....by O.T. Bonnett, M.D.
Why Healing Happens...by O.T. Bonnett, M.D.
A Journey Into Being...by Christine Ramos, RN
Discover The Universe Within You...................................by Mary Letorney
Worlds Beyond Death...by Rev. Grant H. Pealer
Let's Get Natural With Herbs...by Debra Rayburn
The Enchanted Garden..by Jodi Felice
My Teachers Wear Fur Coats..................by Susan Mack & Natalia Krawetz
Seeing True...by Ronald Chapman
Elder Gods of Antiquity...by M. Don Schorn

For more information about any of the above titles, soon to be released titles, or
other items in our catalog, write or visit our website:

OZARK
MOUNTAIN
PUBLISHING

PO Box 754
Huntsville, AR 72740
www.ozarkmt.com
1-800-935-0045/479-738-2348 Wholesale Inquiries Welcome